Dedicated to My Beloved, Sri Sathya Sai Baba,
my Guru, my God and my loving family;
Ma, Prahalad, D'Avery and Deshlin.

Desert Wisdom

Ask Spirit; Feel the Emotions;
Use the Intellect; Then Act.

Vasantha Lakshmi Sai

BALBOA.
PRESS
A DIVISION OF HAY HOUSE

Balboa Press books may be ordered through booksellers or by contacting:

Balboa Press
A Division of Hay House
1663 Liberty Drive
Bloomington, IN 47403
www.balboapress.com.au
1-(877) 407-4847

ISBN: 978-1-4525-0508-4 (sc)
ISBN: 978-1-4525-0509-1 (e)

Printed in the United States of America

Balboa Press rev. date: 08/07/2012

One God Many Forms

Meditation on any form of God is good.

~ Baba ~

There is only one nation,
The nation of humanity
There is only one religion,
The religion of love
There is only one language,
The language of the heart
There is only one God
And He is Omnipresent (Sai Baba)

Contents

Preface

This is an autobiographical account of my spiritual odyssey with Sai Baba, the universal teacher. My relationship with Baba is purely spiritual. I have not met Sai Baba physically, though I was in His presence as one of the many thousands of devotees that attended His birthday celebrations in November 2008.

Bhagawan Sri Sathya Sai Baba has made His advent into this world with a view to raising humanity as a whole to a higher consciousness based on the living faith that all human beings are inherently divine. He seeks not followers, nor for people to change their religious faiths but He does ask that we open to the truth of who we really are.

"I am God," Sri Sathya Sai Baba says in answer to those who question Him about His identity and His miracles. "You are God as well but the only difference between you and me is that I am aware of My Divinity but you are not."

My personal experience with Baba has been through inner messages, dreams, artwork, songs and books. It felt as if Baba said: "Okay, enough floundering in the dark, it is time for some real learning!" And then the games began!!!

At times the learning was so varied that I made no sense of what I was being guided to and through. The books ranged from *A Course in Miracles*, Betty Friedan's *Feminine Mystique*, *The Vedanta, the Upanishads, The Way of Mastery Course, The Gita*, to books on positive thoughts, Lucifer, Sai Teachings, Tantra, Kundalini, biographies of Ghandi and Nelson Mandela, Chakras and many others. This occurred from 2008 to midway 2010. Finally I was given the message to 'connect the dots.' Desert Wisdom is my attempt to connect those dots.

Knowledge can only become personal wisdom when it is experimented with, tested, applied and practised. This I continue to do in my daily life.

Life is not a private affair. A story and its lessons are only made useful when shared. I have chosen to honour my teacher, My Beloved, Sai Baba, by sharing His wisdom; my learning.

Baba wrote this note to Charles Penn, a Sai devotee:

"After long searches here and there, in temples and in churches, in earth and in heavens, at last you come back. Completing the circle from where you started, to your own soul and find that He for whom you have been weeping and praying in churches and temples, on whom you were looking as the mystery of all mysteries shrouded in the clouds in nearest of the near, is your own self, the reality of your life, body and soul. That is your own nature. Assert it, manifest it. It is truth and truth alone, that is one's real friend, relative. Abide by truth; tread the path of righteousness and not a hair of your body will ever be injured. Meditation is nothing else but rising above desires. Renunciation is the power of battling against evil forces and holding the mind in check."
With love and blessings Sri Sathya Sai Baba

I think we are like glasses of lemonade that argue that they are not water but lemon and sugar! Sai Baba says that we are 80% divine and 20% human. For transformation to occur we need to shift our focus from the 20% to the 80%.

Sai Baba Enters

"SAI BABA HAS COME to sit in for your reading," said Olgaa with a surprised smile. "This is the first time this has happened in one of my sessions. Oh, now He wants me to offer you a glass of water."

My eyes flew open and I gasped audibly, for at that exact moment I was overcome by a thirst so great that it felt like I had been walking for miles across an arid desert and had just fallen onto my knees exhausted and dehydrated and very close to death.

My husband and I had gone to Olgaa Fienco for an angel channelling session. Richard, a programmer, was between job contracts and was seeking a new position. He called a former work colleague to confirm his role as a referee and during their brief telephone conversation, Olgaa's name came up and by the end of that short exchange he had booked an appointment for us to see her. Olgaa, the partner of Richard's work colleague, channelled angels and did intuitive readings. I had not met Olgaa or her partner before. I went along with my husband on a trickle of curiosity. For Richard to have booked a session of this type was out of character.

A few days later, I took a deep breath and stepped through Olgaa's front door. After the initial introductions, appropriate small talk and the offering of refreshments which we politely declined, Olgaa ushered us into her lounge where she did her channelling. The first thing that met my eyes was a photograph of Sai Baba on her mantelpiece. Next to Baba were images of Jesus and other angels.

I knew then somewhere deep within that I was meant to be there. I had prayed to Sai Baba for years and my most fervent prayer to Him was to help me improve the communication between my husband and me. I prayed to be a good mother to my two sons and a caring daughter to my mother. But somehow it felt that the more I prayed, the greater were the challenges. Many bad tempered conversations with Him followed. Frankly, I felt that as God and the universal teacher He was failing hopelessly. To say that the relationship between my partner and me was strained would be an euphemism. Furthermore, most of the conversations with my mother, who lived with me, ended up in fits of fury and rants and rages. I felt like a ship lost at sea with its hull being bashed against a powerful iceberg that would not budge.

After I had the drink of water that Olgaa brought to me, we settled into the session once again. My mind was reeling, I was in awe and my scepticism of the authenticity of angel channellers was receding. This time Olgaa was a channel for Sai Baba and Baba had one message for me.

It was: "Read those books."

"What books are these?" I asked.

Baba then showed Olgaa three books and told her that I had them already. He even showed her where they were in my house! Olgaa described them to me and this was how I was led to, *A Course in Miracles*, a book on *Positive Thoughts* and a book on *Sai Teachings*.

I asked Baba for some guidance for my husband and me and according to Olgaa, He held a yellow birthday cake in His hand, smiled mischievously and then left.

At the end of the session, Olgaa gave me a recording of all that she channelled.

The hunger of the mind can be appeased by
the acquisition of knowledge.
Sai Baba

School Starts—A Course in Miracles

I BEGAN MY NIGHTLY READING of passages from *A Course in Miracles.* Now, anyone who has read and studied this book would understand that this was no bedtime reading. I had many impolite conversations with Baba as to why He, an Indian Guru, would see fit to direct me, a Hindu girl to a Christian book, most of which seemed to be too difficult for me to understand anyway.

Listening to the Holy Spirit, the voice of God within is the central teaching in *A Course in Miracles.* Helen Schucman the scribe of the course says, "Its only purpose is to provide a way in which some people will be able to find their own Internal Teacher."

I, however, missed this entire message in my initial reading. The pages were very thin, the writing was very small and the concepts were very difficult for me to assimilate.

My lifestyle was similar to that of many working mothers. It revolved around the children, house and family. Work fitted in there somewhere amidst preparing school lunches, dropping kids at school, dashing off to work, returning home to cook dinner, doing the laundry and seeing to school notices. When I eventually fell exhausted into my bed late at night, I would drag out my copy of *ACIM* and read a few pages at a time.

Most of the time, I felt so sad and lonely. My marriage had reached a point where I had no idea what to do anymore. I had gone for counselling alone. I tried correcting patterns in my behaviour that I identified as being self-defeating. I prayed and cried and prayed some more. All the while I could hear my mother's words ringing in my ears: "A Hindu bride must be the rock in her marriage . . ."

I read and re-read books on love languages and relationship rescues. I tried practising the suggested techniques. Nothing worked. I was in a relationship that had gone awry. A relationship laced with pain, confusion and emptiness. I had lost touch with my own personal power, my own dignity, my standards and my self-esteem. I had lost touch with my core consciousness. I could no longer find nor hear this God-given core in me. I had rationalised away many hopes and dreams and was trying to settle for so many things I did not want.

November 10, 2008, about six months into my study of *ACIM*, was my twenty-fourth wedding anniversary. It is a strange phenomenon that on significant days like Christmas, Diwali, birthdays and anniversaries it is very difficult to be in denial. The truth of your situation threatens to surface and drown you with despair. I, however, had consciously decided that I would get through this day by not acknowledging it. My husband had not been talking to me for a few months and I, who had experienced this silent treatment repeatedly for many years reasoned that this would pass and all I had to do was breathe deeply and be the rock. For many years I would silently sing the words of the song *Smile* to help me through these tough patches. '*Smile when your heart is breaking, Smile when your world is shaking, Smile whenever you're feeling blue . . .*'

However, my best laid plans were not to be that year. My sister, who I had spoken to earlier that day and with whom I shared my intentions of allowing this day to go quietly by, decided to surprise me with an anniversary cake. To say that I was furious would hardly begin to describe the explosive rage that erupted from the very depths of my being.

I went to bed visibly shaking. I was so angry and guilty at the same time. I was also so ashamed at my behaviour. I had allowed my son to see me totally out of control. I was in such anguish. My sister insisted that her intentions were good and she only wanted us to remember the good times. So why was it that her acts of goodness felt so wrong for me?

I awoke the next morning with a strong, clear, urgent inner message to go immediately to the Sai Baba ashram in Puttaparthi. I turned to my husband and told him but he did not even acknowledge hearing me. When he was in silent mode, nothing penetrated his armour. The rest of the family thought I was referring to the Sai centre close to my home in Melbourne. I should mention here that though I spoke to Baba often in my head, I did not go for weekly bhajans nor was I seen as a Sai devotee. Stating that I wanted to go to the ashram was unexpected and was met with bemusement by all.

Assume silence when anger comes into your consciousness, or remember the name of God. Do not remind yourself of things that will inflame the mind and feelings even more.
Sai Baba

Prashanthi Niyalam—Baba's Ashram

THROUGH A SERIES OF events which could only have been orchestrated by the hand of the divine, I arrived in India ten days later, accompanied by my mother. My sister had bought a ticket for my mother so that I would not go to India alone. At this stage I was beyond caring whether she came along or not. I had fought my husband, my sister and my mother for so long. The fight had gone out of me. Besides their arguments that I did not speak Hindi or Tamil and it would be unsafe for a woman to be travelling alone, sounded reasonable.

I arrived in Bangalore around midnight after a very long flight. The hotel I had booked into had arranged a taxi for us and I was pleasantly surprised to see a modern new vehicle. The newly built airport and the modern vehicle were reassuring signs and I wondered sceptically at all those horror stories of filth and squalor I had heard from relatives and friends who had returned from visits to India. I expected a quiet ride to the ashram and hoped to catch up with a bit of sleep before the five o'clock morning prayer.

Soon the sights and sounds assailed me. I was in absolute awe at the total disregard of road rules and all traffic lights. Drivers and riders hooted incessantly as they ignored all red lights. Dogs lay on the roads and narrowly escaped death each time a car came roaring by. I gasped and shrieked in terror. The streets were a thoroughfare for cars, lopsided buses, cows, people, bicycles and bikes carrying entire families. I peered through the night darkness and caught glimpses of road workers, women in saris, carrying large heavy slabs of concrete on their heads. It was one o'clock in the morning.

"Where you from?" asked Dev the taxi driver breaking the silence in the car.

"Australia," I answered distractedly not daring to take my eyes off the road.

"You don't look Australian," he said.

"Oh, I was born in South Africa," I replied.

"You don't look African," he persisted.

Finally I gave in and gave him the answer he sought.

"I am Indian."

That pleased him.

"You Hindu?" he asked.

"Yes."

"Very good, me too, I Hindu," he smiled. "You got husband? Which God you pray to? How many children you got?" I glanced at my mother, my interpreter, but she was sound asleep beside me.

The barrage of questions continued for the next hour until we reached the hotel, Sai Towers, at 2am.

The moment I stepped out of the taxi I was overcome by deep feelings of sadness and tears rolled freely and shamelessly down my cheeks. I felt like a young child who had bruised herself in a fall and had fled crying into the arms of her mother for comforting and healing.

My journey, with Sai Baba running through it all like a golden thread, continued . . .

A Guru does not teach anything new,
he reveals you to yourself.
Sai Baba

A Bit About Me

My name is Vasantha, which means spring or new beginnings. I am the third girl born into our family. It had been told in jest on many occasions that my father walked into the maternity ward when I was born, took one look at me, heard I was a girl and then walked straight out again. He had wanted a boy.

My mother, who was struggling to make ends meet on my father's meagre salary, could not afford to have another child. According to Ma, Pa drank through much of his youth and that buggered his livers. Pa, however, was a gentle man who never raised his voice nor hands to his three daughters or my mother.

My mother, an intelligent woman, was forced to leave school when she was in grade five and was put to work on the family farm. This she did with her sister for about fifteen years. When the farm was sold due to the shocking impact of the Group Areas Act in Apartheid South Africa, the two unmarried sisters who had been the convenient unpaid farm workers were then inconvenient financial burdens.

The income that the farm generated went mostly to the head of the family, the oldest son. The patriarchal system existed and persisted very strongly in our family. It was the 1950's. Feminism had not reached those shores. Since the girls were not needed on the farm anymore it was decided by the older sons that it was time to marry them off.

Marriages were soon arranged. My mother and aunt, who were in their late twenties, were already regarded as spinsters in their community and the hot African sun had not been kind to their skins and complexions. Girls with smooth fair skins were the preferred choice. My aunt was married to a twice-divorced man, a fact she only learnt on her wedding day. My mother married my father who was ten years her senior and because of various maladies was unable to work regularly.

By the time I was seven months old, my mother had to go out to work to support the family and bring in a steady income. She found employment as a machinist in a clothing factory. Ma worked very long hours, often seven days a week. She left home at sunrise when we were still asleep and would frequently return very late in the evenings.

Children are notoriously oblivious to the truth of their surroundings. Two strong women took care of my sisters and me. Ayah, my grandmother and Mummy, my aunt were our surrogate mothers. We were fed, clothed, bathed, taken care of when ill and a ready smack was available when we were naughty. The concerns of adults did not affect us. I felt safe, happy and carefree.

I whiled away the hours of each day happily and contentedly. I played with dolls and tea-sets with my sisters. For many hours I would play tunes on a recorder and pretend that I was Krishna. I loved the sound of music and I composed many musical tunes on the recorder. I played hopscotch, cops and robbers, hide and seek and skipping games with the children in the neighbourhood. There seemed to be children all around us. I raced with the neighbourhood boys and my cousins, along the streets, and developed my sprinting abilities. We journeyed through the bushy undergrowth that was our backyard like intrepid explorers. We would reach the mango tree, sit under the lush growth of wild creepers and feast on juicy yellow mangoes. Other days we would sneak into the neighbour's backyard, steal sugar-canes from the garden and devour these surreptitiously. What fun! What delight! My love affair with sugar must surely have started here. Mr Singh, the neighbour, was always on the watchout and he would yell obscenities at us from his upstairs window when he caught us and then our backsides would sting and roaring parents caused momentary deafness.

I loved and delighted in my adventures with the boys that were fraught with scratches and bruises as much as I loved the gentle and imaginary games I played with the girls.

My life flowed from an adventure filled childhood to a carefree adolescence. I loved music, singing, sports, dressing in my mother's creations and boys. Academically I didn't do too badly so I had no real hiccoughs.

My best friend in primary school was a Muslim girl, called Rookhaya. From her I learnt about Allah, Eid and Madrasas. In high school, Jennet, a devout Christian, and I were inseparable. Religion is no barrier in the innocence and purity of childhood and youth.

I met my husband by the time I was 18 and was married before I was 21. He answered many of a young girl's fantasy. He was intelligent and handsome, rode a bike, was a pilot, had travelled to many different parts of the world and he loved me.

So how did I come to be where I was when I reached the doorstep of Baba? Why had conventional wisdom failed me so miserably? All my beliefs and assumptions were being shaken at its core and I was totally bewildered by it all. I was 44.

Mothers should be seen worshipping at the altar, meditating in silence, sympathising with pain and grief. They should not be seen by their children as worried, helpless, discontented, and distressed, as if they have no God to lean upon, no inner reserves of strength and courage to fall back upon.
Sai Baba

Back to Prashanthi

My mother and I rested for about an hour, and then awoke to shower and dress for subrapatham, the morning prayer that is sung before sunrise to awaken the Gods. I walked around the ashram in the early hours of the morning, with hundreds of devotees of all nationalities. We were at the ashram during Sai Baba's birthday celebrations. It was 22 November 2008. Since I did not know the words of any of the songs, I prayed quietly and tried my best to join in when I could.

After the morning prayer, we returned to our hotel room, had breakfast and then prepared to return for the nine o'clock darshan. Darshan was when Baba came to the temple and blessed all those present with His presence.

I stepped out of the hotel, erroneously thinking that since I was an hour early I had ample time to get a good seat in the ashram. We were confronted with throngs of people. I was astounded by the thousands lining up waiting for the doors to open. The queues stretched endlessly around the extensive buildings. Most waited patiently for an opportunity to see Baba. Some however, cut into the long queues. The older Indian women were notorious for this. I observed this all quietly from my place in the line. Men and women in uniform walked about idly without really enforcing much discipline. I was fascinated to see the police women wearing saris as their uniforms. I wore saris on special occasions, usually with great ceremony and even greater discomfort. I tried to find a place for my 80 year old mother to sit but she too had to move as the queue moved. Old and young, sick and healthy, rich and poor, no-one was special. All were eagerly awaiting entrance into the temple-hall.

As we got closer to the doors, all semblance of order was lost and we became a sea of bodies being sucked into the mouth of the temple. Trying to yell out, "Stop pushing," had no effect at all. When we gave in to that force and became one with the flow and stopped worrying about being trampled to death, we were carried through the door. My first lesson in surrender began.

We were seated by the sevadas, volunteer workers. Any misconceptions I might have had about having some personal space quickly vanished. Every centimetre of floor space was occupied. When I thought it was not possible to fit in another body, we were asked to move by the sevadas and a whole new row of people were seated. Thousands of us huddled together in the November heat straining our necks as we waited expectantly for Sai Baba's arrival.

Soon there was a stir and buzz in the crowd. The regular temple goers seemed to know something but since this was my first time in the ashram I had no idea what to expect. Then Baba was driven into the hall and wheeled out in a wheel-chair.

How can I describe in words what I felt? I can't really but I will attempt to do so. The cells in my body seemed to fill up with something and expand. I shuddered and trembled and then the tears rose from the depths of my being. I sobbed uncontrollably. After some moments had passed, I glanced sideways and saw an old lady pleading silently and earnestly to Baba and she had tears rolling down her face too. So I know I was not alone in feeling what I did.

Baba's presence is palpable. So much love and devotion was present in that room. Thousands of people from all over the world were crammed close together all hoping for a brief glimpse of Sai Baba. I recalled the words of Sai Baba where He says that His love for the most devout devotee is no greater than His love for the worst sinner. This reassured me, because I certainly was no devout devotee.

For while I prayed to Baba I knew there were lots of doubts and gaps in my faith.

The present is a product of the past,
but it is also the seed for the future.
Sai Baba

Sri Sathya Sai Baba

"I AM GOD. AND YOU too are God. The only difference between you and Me is that while I am aware of it, you are completely unaware." This is the answer Bhagawan Sri Sathya Sai Baba gives to people who query Him about His identity and divinity. This fundamental truth of man's divine nature is at the heart of His message and mission. Indeed, in His discourses to devotees, He addresses them as "Embodiments of the Divine Atma". All who experience His pure and selfless love, and benefit from His illuminating counsel, and witness His miraculous nature get a glimpse of the glory and majesty of God, and therefore of what one potentially and inherently is.

Sri Sathya Sai Baba was born as Sathyanarayana Raju on November 23, 1926 in the village of Puttaparthi, in the state of Andhra Pradesh in South India. Even as a child, His spiritual inclination and contemplative nature set Him apart from other children of His age, and He was known as 'Guru' and "Brahmajnani' (knower of Brahman or Godhead) among His peers and others in the village. However, it was not until October 20, 1940, the day He made the historic declaration of His Avatarhood, (Avatar-Divinity Incarnate) that the world at large learnt of this divine phenomenon.

Elucidating on His mission, Bhagawan declares, "I have come not to disturb or destroy any faith, but to confirm each in his own faith, so that the Christian becomes a better Christian, the Muslim a better Muslim and the Hindu a better Hindu." His formula for man to lead a meaningful life is the five-fold path of Sathya (Truth), Dharma (Righteousness), Shanthi (Peace), Prema (Love) and Ahimsa (Non-Violence). Love for God, fear of sin and morality in society; these are His prescriptions for our ailing world.

In a divine discourse given by Baba on 'Why He incarnates', Baba says:

> *For the protection of the virtuous, for the destruction of evil-doers, and for establishing righteousness on a firm footing, I incarnate from age to age. Whenever ashanthi or disharmony, overwhelms the world, the Lord will incarnate in human form to establish the modes of earning prashanti, or peace, and to re-educate the human community in the paths of peace.*
>
> *At the present time, strife and discord have robbed peace and unity from the family, the schools, the communities, societies, villages, cities and states. The arrival of the Lord is also anxiously awaited by the saints and the sages. Sadhus prayed, and I have come. My main tasks are fostering of the Vedas and fostering of the devotees. Your virtue, your self-control, your detachment, your faith, your steadfastness—these are the signs in which people read of my glory.*
>
> *You can lay claim to be My devotee only when you have placed yourself in My hands fully and completely with no trace of ego. The Avatar behaves in a human way so that mankind can feel kinship, but rises into his superhuman heights so that mankind can aspire to reach heights and through that aspiration can actually reach Him.*
>
> *Realising the Lord within you as the motivator is the task for which He comes in human form. Avatars like Krishna and Rama had to kill one or more individuals who could be identified as enemies of the dharmic way of life and thus restore the practice of virtue. But now there is no-one fully good. And so, who deserves the protection of the Lord? All are tainted by wickedness, and so who will survive if this Avatar decides to uproot? Therefore, I have come to correct the 'buddhi' the intelligence by various*

means. I have to counsel, help, command, condemn, and stand by as a friend and well-wisher to all, so that they may give up evil propensities and recognising the straight path, tread it and reach the goal. I have to reveal to the people the worth of the Vedas, the Shastras, and other spiritual texts which lay down the norms. If you accept Me and say 'Yes,' I too respond and say 'Yes.' If you deny and say 'No,' I also echo 'No.' Come, examine, experience, and have faith. That is the method of utilising Me.

I do not mention about Sai Baba in any of My discourses. Though I bear the name as Avatar of Sai Baba, I do not appreciate in the least the distinction between the various appearances of God—Sai, Rama, Krishna, etc—I do not proclaim that this is more important or that the other is less important. Continue your worship of your chosen God along the lines already familiar to you. Then you will find that you are coming nearer and nearer to me, for all names are mine and all forms are mine. There is no need to change your chosen God and adopt a new one when you have seen Me or heard Me.

Every step in the career of the Avatar is predetermined. Rama came to feed the roots of Sathya, or Truth, and Dharma, righteousness. Krishna came to foster Shanti-peace and Prema, love. Now all these four are in danger of being dried up. That is why the present Avatar has come. The Dharma that has fled to forests has to be led back into the villages and towns. The anti-dharma that is ruining the villages and towns has to be driven into the jungle.

I have come to give you the keys of the treasure of Ananda, or bliss, to tell you how to tap that spring, for you have forgotten the way to blessedness. If you waste this chance of saving yourselves, it is just your fate. You have come to get from Me tinsels and trash, the petty little cures and promotions, worldly joy and comforts. Very few of you, desire to get from Me the thing I have come to give you, namely, liberation itself. Even among these few those who stick to the path of Sadhana, or spiritual practice, and succeed, are a handful.

Your worldly intelligence cannot fathom the ways of God. He cannot be recognised by mere intelligence. You may benefit from God, but you cannot explain Him. Your explanations are mere guesses, attempts to cloak your ignorance in pompous expressions. Bring something into your daily practice as evidence of your having known that secret of the higher life from Me. Show that you have greater brotherliness, speak with more sweetness and self-control. Bear defeat as well as victory with calm resignation.

The establishment of dharma-righteousness that is My aim. The teachings of dharma, the spread of dharma that is My object.

My task is not merely to cure and console and remove individual misery; but something far more important. The removal of misery and distress is incidental to My mission. My main task is the re-establishment of Vedas and Shastras and revealing the knowledge about them to all people. This task will succeed. When the Lord decides and wills, His Divine will cannot be hindered.

I have come to instruct all in the essence of the Vedas, to shower on all, this precious gift, to protect Sanatana Dharma—the ancient wisdom—and preserve it. My mission is to spread happiness, and so I am always ready to come among you, not once, but twice and thrice, as often as you want Me.

Many of you come to Me with problems of help and mental worry of some sort or the other. They are mere baits by which you have been brought here. The main purpose is that you may have the grace of God and strengthen your faith in the Divine. Problems and worries are merely to be welcomed as they teach you lessons in humility and reverence.

I know the agitations of your heart and its aspirations, but you do not know my heart. I react to the pain that you undergo and to the joy that you feel, for I am in your heart. I am the dweller in the temple of every heart. Do not lose contact and company, for it is only when the lump of coal is in contact with the live ember that it can also become a live ember. Cultivate nearness to me in your heart and you will be rewarded. *Then you too will acquire a fraction of supreme love. This is a great chance. Be confident that you will be liberated. Know that you are saved. Many hesitate to believe that things will improve, that life will be happy for all and full of joy, and that the golden age will recur. Let Me assure you that this Dharmaswarupa, this Divine body has not come in vain. It will succeed in warding off crisis that has come upon humanity.*

Sathya Sai Baba

There is no need to exhaust yourselves with the search for God. He is there like butter in milk, like a chicken in an egg, in every atom of creation. He does not come from somewhere or go somewhere. He is here, there and everywhere. From the atom to the cosmos, from the microcosm to the macrocosm. He is everything.
Sai Baba

Return to Prashanthi

THE FIVE DAYS SPENT at the ashram saw my emotions waver from intense devotion and deep inner peace and love, to overwhelming feelings of sadness and moments when my over-active mind just would not stop. I wondered why the westerners, the Sai group from Italy were being given special privileges. They were allowed to sit close to Baba and received special saris from Him. I knew feelings of envy and jealousy were arising and I tried to quell them but they refused to be stifled. Then I wished that I could be closer to the stage, only to find the next day I was even further away. However, the view of Baba was better. The third day, the day of Baba's birthday I was much further away. I was, in fact, right out of the hall in the glaring November sun and this was when my view of Baba was the clearest with the least amount of obstructions.

On the fourth and fifth days, the days after Baba's birthday I had a profound experience and I knew then that Baba is indeed omnipresent and is aware at all times of us, His children. He communicated with me via another Sai devotee from Russia who is an open channel to the divine. That experience touched me deeply. While India was being terrorised with bombings at several well-known hotels, I experienced a love so great, so intense, and so profound that I am at a loss to describe it.

And so I had my second 'interview' with Sai Baba. I received the answer I required.

During the flight back to Melbourne, I glanced across at my mother who was reading a Mills and Boon, took a much needed breath and announced, "I'm leaving, Ma. It's over. I can't do this anymore."

"What! No, you can't, what would happen to the children?" she asked. She knew immediately what I was referring to.

"They're hardly children at 21 and 16," I sighed.

"What would people think?" she argued.

"I'm past caring about that, Ma."

"How would you afford to live?" she demanded.

"I work, Ma," I reminded her. "I'll find a way."

"What is a woman without a man? A woman needs a man to have respect. I stayed with your father even though I was not happy," she continued.

My resolve to stay calm was fast diminishing. And so the argument went on, with her trying desperately to convince me to stay in a marriage that had become so dysfunctional.

Once the decision that I found so difficult to make, was made, I felt a deep sense of stillness. I would like to say that my husband was devastated and pleaded with me to stay, but that would be my pride and ego trying to stay intact. The actual separation and divorce took over a year but through it all I felt like I was being carried on God's shoulders. The Westlife song, *You raise me up* comforted me. The words of this song spoke directly to my heart. I knew I was being guided and protected as I moved through a maze of unknowns.

You are My life, My breath, My soul. You are My forms, all. When I love you, I love Myself; when you love yourselves, you love Me. I separated Myself from Myself, so that I may love Myself. My beloved ones, you are My own Self.
Sai Baba

Dreams

I HAD ALWAYS BEEN A dreamer, both during the nights and days
even though my mother told me often when I was a little girl that
dreams and daydreams were just useless fantasies and don't mean
much. As I grew older the dreams lessened and then became almost
non-existent.

After the trip to India I started to dream prolifically. I began
having series of dreams each night. Soon I was dreaming more
than I was sleeping or rather that's what it felt like. The dreams
seemed to have themes to them. I went through many dreams having
showers or baths. Then I found myself having to use the toilet in
the dreams. Soon I was vacuuming, gardening, looking for keys
and crystals, driving home on freeways with my eyes closed—this
terrified me. I had many erotic dreams. I also had many powerful
dreams with Sai Baba, Mother Mary and Jesus in them. I seemed to
be asking, demanding, fighting, pleading and looking for someone
or something. Often I dreamt about family members.

Soon I started to notice that some dreams were prophetic dreams.
Some of the dreams were about events in books or the plot lines of
films that I had not read nor seen at the time of the dream. Other
times I dreamt about conversations and events that unfolded later. I
always had the dream first then the experience.

I was guided, via inner communication to write the dreams
down, so I did. Within a year I had filled four large notebooks. One

morning, Selvie, a dear cousin, was walking her dog when a book on dreams caught her eye. She told me that she knew she had to get this book for me. So she returned home, got her bag then went back to the shop to buy the dream book.

Connie Kaplan in her book; *The Woman's Book of Dreams— Dreaming as a spiritual practice* states: The Truth presents itself in dreaming and later exposes itself in form. The dreamer must simply learn to read the signs and track the energy. Truth is not just a noun but a dimension—a dreaming dimension. In the dreaming of truth, one is in direct relationship with energy without the restraints of personal will or social laws. The need for something to make sense no longer exists. Truth is boundless. The opposite of truth is not 'lies' but rather a sense of separation. Truth does not exist in the realm of language. Real truth exists in one's ability to move into its dimension.

This book helped me understand what I was experiencing. I had read many books on dream interpretation but they had not provided me with the answers I needed.

In August 2008, I was referred to an obstetrician by my doctor because I was unwell. I just assumed it was stress related, so for a long time I ignored the symptoms. Blood tests were taken and my iron levels were found to be very low and the constant pain I was experiencing was due to a prolapsed womb. I had severe blood loss during menstruation, and could hardly move myself about, during the first three days. This combined with already low iron levels left me feeling desperately ill. I took the letter of referral and went to the specialist, who did the usual preliminary examinations then asked, "What is your age?"

"44," I replied.

"Do you have children?" he asked.

"Yes," I replied.

"Do you want any more children?" he asked.

"No," I said.

"I think the best thing to do is a hysterectomy," he said. "You won't have any problems with excessive bleeding, your iron levels will be restored and it lowers the risk of uterus cancer."

This all sounded very sensible to me and fifteen minutes into that consultation I agreed to the operation and was even booked in for surgery within the next few weeks. But when I got home I suddenly knew deep within me that I could not have the hysterectomy. My logical mind tried to argue that this would make me feel better, but a voice far stronger was saying NO. It felt like some ancient memory had been stirred but I did not know what it was. I cancelled the operation.

I learnt, almost two years later, that some women are born with the gift of dreaming and that the womb is the dreaming organ. Dreaming comes through the internal, secret knowledge of the womb. There are subtle energies connected to a woman's womb that she does not necessarily understand unless she goes through exhaustive training with a female shaman or sorcerer. Just as a woman who gives birth to a child does not know the biological processes in the womb that create the child, neither does she fully understand the subtle spiritual dreaming energy connected to the womb. In addition, there is a sacred connection between a woman and the moon. The moon controls the woman's cycles just as it controls the ocean's tides. The ocean is Mother Earth's cyclical waters and the menstrual blood is women's.

When my husband and I built our dream home in 2003, I recall as part of the speech at the housewarming party, I said that I had the dream and my husband made it a reality and that was how it was for so many things in our life. But as I uttered those words it felt like I was having an outer body experience and was watching me speak. I certainly hadn't thought about it consciously. Later, I learnt that according to ancient teachings given to dreaming women that was a key axiom.

Women are the life givers. Men are the life-makers. Women dream the dream and give the gift. Men manifest and focus the dream. Of course, we are all created from the same energy, and we all return to the same energy. But in the dimension of physical existence, we live primarily as either male or female. Our attempts to balance the masculine and feminine within ourselves and our relationships can be the richest and sometimes, as I found, the most painful experiences of our lives. As dreamers it is essential to keep masculine and feminine energies balanced. We are accountable for the imbalance our world seems to experience today, and we must work tirelessly to create a new balance. Since we are responsible for the dream, it is our sacred duty to free ourselves from blocks to our visions. Emotions held in our bodies block dreaming and prevent us from owning our power.

As we dream, we are also being dreamed by an unfathomable intelligence, God. Dreamers must realise that they are being dreamed by a larger, more omniscient energy than themselves. God is the matrix of the universe that holds all creation. That matrix is an invisible force, the Spirit that motivates creation and evokes evolution. We are indeed nourished by the unseen as well as the seen. If, as a dreaming woman, I can understand myself as an extension of that matrix, I can then begin to remember who I am in the story of creation. God simultaneously feeds us dream information and receives our dreams. She and we are part of the wholeness of the universe.

God is dreaming a change in consciousness at this time in our evolution. She is giving us all the assistance and information we need in our dreaming. However, we must receive it, perceive it and put it to work. We are birthing ourselves into a new species. Dreaming is our midwife.

While some of us are born as dreamers and this assists in our awakening to the truth, all of us can use questions and answers to remind ourselves of the truth of who we are.

Socrates, a realised soul and great philosopher, believed in the reincarnation of an eternal soul which contained all knowledge. We unfortunately lose touch with that knowledge at every birth, and so rather than learning something new, we need to be reminded of what we already know. Socrates said that he did not teach, but rather served, like his mother, as a midwife to truth that is already in us! He made use of questions and answers to remind his students of knowledge. This is called maieutics, midwifery.

In 2008 I had the urge to have another baby. I could not understand this deep longing within me, especially at a time when my relationship was so troubled and I was sterilised. Soon I started to crave certain foods. I ate whole lettuces and bottles of olives daily. I also had the strangest urge to suck on Eno antacid powder nightly. It was bizarre. This went on for almost the entire year.

After returning from India, I had sensations in my stomach of a baby moving inside. They were very visible movements. I was going through all the symptoms that I had when I was pregnant with my two sons. Psychologists would describe what I was going through as a psycho-somatic illness or a phantom pregnancy but I knew it was much more than this. I had read that sometimes people have spontaneous kundalini awakenings and I figured that that must be what was happening to me. I had no real knowledge of what exactly the kundalini was but it was written that this is very dangerous without the guidance of a proper guru so I decided not to delve on this any further. After many months of experiencing these physical symptoms, my dreams then had babies in them. I was usually holding the baby and cooking at the same time. One day, as I was having this strange experience, I opened a Sai Baba book and in it Baba taps His stomach and laughingly tells a devotee that He is pregnant, He is birthing Prema, Love. This felt like a message for me. Was I too birthing a new energy? The energy of love. As I reflect on this now, it feels like I was giving birth and being birthed into a new being. It feels like I have literally dreamt myself awake only to awaken to the reality that I had never been asleep.

Unity; Purity; Divinity
Sai Baba

My Initiation and The Rainbow Serpent

On 20 March 2010, I received a remote energetic healing transmission from Padma Aon, to release karmic knots. That night I had a powerful dream.

> *I go to a snake park with three snakes in a cat basket. When I get there the snakes are let loose and I notice them winding around each other. Soon I am unable to tell my snakes apart from the ones in the snake park. I get worried and anxious. Then a relative appears in the dream and she tells me to, 'ask the man.' I turn around and notice the curator of the snake park. She speaks to him in an ancient language (seems like Tamil and Aboriginese) and I wonder how she knows this language. Then I remember that she is a great scholar and she must have learnt it at some time. She relays to me that I must go to a sacred site to pray and then I will get the snakes back. I do. When I return I see my snakes but I am afraid to put them into the basket because their heads are up and they look quite aggressive. I ask my mother for help, but she is afraid. So I do it myself, Steve Ervin style! Then I notice one thick long beautiful snake and I think that this is one of the original three that has grown. The curator says that he will keep that one. I think that he wants to keep it to show the others. It is a detached observation. I have three snakes in the cat basket that look the same as the original three, only they are different.*

A few weeks later I met my cousin, the one in the dream, at a friend's wake and I told her about the dream. She immediately identified the colourful snake as the Rainbow Serpent. When I got home, I googled *Rainbow Serpent*. The results came up with Ayers Rock. In Uluru, Ayers Rock is called the Rainbow Serpent. It is a sacred site in the shape of a woman's womb and was a significant site for Aboriginal Dreaming Woman.

My pulse started to race and my entire body vibrated with the urgency to go there. I had to be there by the 28th April 2010, the following week. This made no sense to me. I certainly had no desire to go to Ayers Rock and I had only just learnt what the Rainbow Serpent was.

In the Aboriginal Dreamtime Stories the Rainbow Serpent is said to be the original God who birthed the world, the mountains, rivers, people, plants, and insects.

Later that evening, I looked at my sons across the dinner table and wondered how I would let them know that their mother was now thinking of going to Uluru because of a dream she had and the energy she was feeling! I had already been to India because of a thought in my head. I decided on a casual approach.

"I'm thinking of going to Ayers Rock next week," I slipped this into the conversation casually hoping they were not really listening so that later I could say, "I told you but you were not paying attention as usual!" Only this was not to be.

"What?" they echoed in unison.

"I am thinking of going to Ayers Rock," I repeat, wondering why they would be listening today.

"Ayers Rock? Why?"

"Oh, you remember the dream I . . . . well I'm not quite sure, I just know that I must go there," I say quietly.

I think when we answer the voice of God, God holds your family very closely in His arms. Both the boys were very supportive and encouraged me to go and did not question their mother's sanity even though I certainly was. Leaving Deshlin who was in Year 12 was not something I wanted to be doing.

I tried finding a spiritual tour but could not, so I booked a four day camping tour.

"Camping!" exclaimed D'Avery, my elder son. "Mum, you know you hate camping."

"Yes, well they promised luxury camping," I said, "besides this one feels right for me." I rationalised that since I would be on walks and tours all day, when I got to camp I would be too exhausted to worry about where I put my head down for the night.

Sometimes we need to listen to our children.

I got to Ayers Rock on the 28th of April and decided to go straight to the rock to meditate. I had arranged to join the tour group the following day. When I got to the rock in the midday heat, I walked around the base and tried to find a suitable spot but found barriers around the rock and warning signs forbidding entry and photography. I was not interested in the photographs but I did want to meditate in the sacred female site. I crossed the barrier and sat behind a rock and prayed and hoped that no-one could see me. Tourists were passing by all the time and I could barely concentrate. I did not feel any strong energy at the site nor did I have any wondrous experiences!

"What were you expecting, Vasi?" I asked myself. "The Oracle at Ayers Rock?" I received a lesson on letting go of expectations. I walked away from the rock smiling gently at my silly behaviour.

A few hours later I watched the sunset over Ayers Rock. I sat on a concrete bench and observed a little child playing. The thought passed through my mind that the mother, who was sitting to the right of me, a young Indian woman, was so loving and patient. Then I started a conversation with the lady who was sitting to the left of me. She turned out to be a South African Afrikaaner who was on her way back from India. She had been to an ashram there. During that short exchange she told me that she had been initiated by her guru ten years ago and she touched her forehead with her thumb in an initiatory gesture. I noted the coincidence of me, a South African of Indian descent, now living in Australia, having on either side of me an Indian woman and a South African lady while watching the sunset over Ayers Rock in Australia. It was the 28th of April 2010, a full moon night.

When I got back to the hotel, I knew that exchange was significant and I had the urge to speak to Hazel again. Hazel lived in Johannesburg but we had not shared contact details so I figured that that was unlikely to happen because she had mentioned that she was leaving the next morning.

I lay on my bed and decided to meditate but promptly fell asleep. I was exhausted after the early start and the long walk around the rock.

Around 2am I awoke with the clear message that I was being initiated.

"Initiated?" I gasped. "Whatever does that mean?"

I had no idea what I was being initiated for or into. I was in Ayers Rock because of a dream, the Rainbow Serpent and because very cell in my body had vibrated with the urgency to go there. Then that? Initiation? I was seriously considering the state of my sanity at that point. So, I had a word with Sai Baba in my mind and told him that if I was being initiated and I had heard Him correctly then I would meet Hazel again. Once I made the deal, I calmed down and fell into a deep sleep until 9.30am the following morning. I was joining the tour group at 1pm.

After a quick shower I decided to I visit the Ayers Rock shopping centre before joining the group. I browsed about idly then bought a postcard to send home to my boys. It was one reflecting the moods of the rock.

The Rock represents us as spiritual beings. The Aborigine elders ask that we look beyond the form, within the rock to see its spirit, its source, its essence. Similarly, Jeshua teaches that we need to see from the form to the formless. This was a practice He did when he was a student. We then come to realise that all comes from the same source, the unfathomable one. The spirit, the formless within, is not seen but is there if we stop and listen.

The moods of the rock represent our emotions. Just as the colours of the rock changes depending on the time of day and the environmental conditions so too do humans experience changing emotions depending on circumstances, internal and external conditions. As we notice and appreciate the different hues, each one as beautiful as the next, so too should we, as humans, observe and witness our changing moods. Accept this as innocently as God intended.

The Rock itself is our mind, the intellect which must be as solid as a rock. Our faith must be unwavering like a rock. It should be able to withstand all external conditions.

This is a sacred site because it represents the relationship between man and nature. It is a lesson, a reminder, a teaching from the divine. Divine Guidance given to us through God's creation. Another reminder of who we are.

I was busy writing the above words which seemed to be flowing through me, on the postcard, when I noticed out the corner of my eye someone sit at the table next to mine. It was Hazel.

Tears flowed from my eyes as I once again witnessed Sai Baba's love, power and mystery. Hazel was on her way to the airport and had stopped for a cup of coffee.

Sai Baba often refers to people from the same country as sisters and brothers. Hazel, a South African is from my birthplace. Baba sent my 'sister' to give me the message and confirmation of the initiation.

She later sent me this definition for the word. The meaning of the word initiation is so vast that if it were to be fully expanded it would encompass the whole world, but if it were contracted, then it would merely mean an introduction, a start. Our spiritual progress really begins the moment the Master allows His life impulse to focus on us.

I joined the tour group at one o'clock. The next few days were so surreal and it would be easy to dismiss them as just my imagination, only I know it wasn't.

During the sunrise tour we watched the sun rise in the east and to the west was the full moon still shining brightly in the sky. The feminine lunar and the masculine solar. The God and the Goddess in their full glory smiling down at us. I, together with many other tourists, stood in the centre. It was so spectacular, so magical, so powerful, and so beautiful. It was a shower of blessing to all those who stood on that viewing platform. I stood silently in the midst of the clicking cameras and hushed conversations and breathed deeply and marvelled at God's grandeur.

Later that day, we spotted a little lizard in a circle of small stones. It looked like a sacred circle. Then I observed and recognised images from many dreams that I had in the past. Was I remembering something? Had I been there before, in another life? Were my dreams prophetic? I'm not sure. We also saw two snakes. One crossing the road and another crossed our pathway. I felt like I was living the dream. God's presence was right there, all around waiting to be noticed and greeted. Our tour ended on Anzac Hill, in Alice Springs, with the words 'lest we forget.' Significant words for dreaming women who are reminded to 'remember to remember.' Anzac Hill is a sacred Aborigine site that was home to a lone dreaming woman.

Our tour guide held deep prejudices stemming from ignorance and fears against the people of the land and while he did not say anything explicitly, the commentaries and his dismissive tone regarding the Dreamtime stories revealed this. He criticised the government for giving the elders a say in policy making, he criticised the parks board for listening to the people who claimed rights to the land and he had no idea that Ayers Rock is called the Rainbow Serpent. Neither did he know the story of the Rainbow Serpent even though he was a guide for 15 years. However, he did tell us some stories about early explorers which were of interest and I felt that this was a lesson for me too.

One explorer made several attempts to reach the Olgas. The Olgas are beautifully formed hills in Uluru. This explorer wanted to lay claim to it, as being the first one there. This would have gained him fame and fortune in England. However, due to an unforeseen delay, someone else beat him to it and he was outraged at having lost this opportunity, especially as he was so convinced that he was the only one pursuing that trail.

Once again I felt that Our Father was sending me a message, a teaching, and using pioneers this time. Pioneers started off as genuine seekers of knowledge, having a deep thirst to quench. They stepped courageously into the unknown. They faced the uncertainty with trepidation but fascination. Many lost their way and some lost their lives; other times they returned to write about indescribable beauty, abundance and un-limitedness. However, soon it became a race to see who got there first. Who got the sponsors? Whose name would be listed as the conqueror? The ego took control. So a genuine need to know changed into a battle of the egos.

Like the pioneers who sought new territories, many of us are seeking, often unconsciously, new knowledge or ancient wisdom. That is what is being revealed to all who learn to listen with a pure heart. However, we must be mindful of our egos and the need to be seen as better or special. So there is a need to go into prayer often and the hedges need to be trimmed. We need to maintain a balance between confidence and humility.

When the four day tour ended and I got to my hotel in Alice Springs, I sank into a comfortable couch and sighed in gratitude. As much as I enjoyed the landscapes and the friendships that were formed I do love a soft warm bed. I wondered yet again if I had just imagined the last few days.

Then a voice came into my head and said, "Go to your e-mail!" It sounded quite stern as if disapproving of the doubts that were arising yet again.

"Go to my e-mail? Here?" I questioned.

I went over to the front desk and enquired about internet access. Soon I was seated in front of a computer, deleting the many e-mails I had not responded to over the past 5 days. Then a new e-mail came through. I gasped in astonishment. It was from a woman in the United States, Carol Marie, who was answering an inner call and was walking across a desert in Arizona following the Rainbow Serpent energy. Both she and I were doing the same thing in two different parts of the world. She was more articulate about what she was doing. I seemed to have blindfolds on.

How did this connection come about? How did she get my e-mail address? Where were the strong inner messages coming from? I have no way of knowing how this happens, I just know that it does and it did.

I had chills running through my body. I immediately forwarded this e-mail to my sons. My need to provide evidence to support what I was saying and experiencing was still strong and this way I could show them the date and time that it had come through.

It is said that the Rainbow has always been the bridge between matter and spirit in many traditions. The Rainbow Serpent and what has been spoken of in legend and myth as the Phoenix have merged into a singular presence to bring balance and harmony within the duality.

That night I had another powerful dream with Sai Baba in it. He smiled happily at my son, Deshlin and tapped him on his head and said that he was Rama. It felt like He wanted to say more but then He smiled and shook His head happily. He also blessed my sister and said that He would remove nine years of bad luck. I asked Him a question in the dream and desperately sought an answer but He looked deep into my eyes and did not answer me. He then turned into a scorpion-like creature and moved away.

The next day, I was due to fly home but had a few hours before the flight so I went into the city centre. As I approached the main street, I noticed a colourful procession of floats. Alice Springs was celebrating May Day. It started off as cattle muster fifty years ago and has now evolved into a community affair. The theme was 'Our Oneness, Our Connectedness, and Our Rainbow Nation as a World.' I was so overwhelmed by this message and my soul cried deeply at God's power and the realisation that we all want the same thing, a return to Oneness; One God, One world. Fear and ignorance have kept us apart for too long. Humanity longs, yearns for this togetherness, this love, this return to wholeness.

On a personal level this seven day trip to Central Australia, desert country, sacred, ancient land, felt like Sai Baba putting on a show just for me. I felt honoured, loved and cherished. I have no way of explaining the mystery and the many miracles that unfolded. All I know is that it happened and I have to somehow quieten this mind of mine that is constantly looking for proof and evidence and forever doubts. I had huge fears which I had to overcome and I am sure more will surface where I thought there were none, but as long as I am having this human experience I am dependent on God—Sai Baba to guide my learning and my learning will be my teaching as my teaching is my learning.

As I took this trip into Central Australia I became deeply aware of the wisdom of the desert. I was visiting an outback cattle station when I noticed a mini-bus with the words *Desert Tracks* on it. Beneath were the words: 'Spirit, emotion, intellect, task'

The previous day a thought had popped into my head that I must write. I immediately dismissed this as ridiculous. Write? Yeah right! This certainly was not one of the things on my bucket list.

Then when I saw these words it came to me that this would be the title of the book. So there I was with a book title but still unsure about what to write.

When I went to Bali three weeks later I sat next to an author during the flight and we spoke all through the trip. When the flight ended she gave me her contact details and invited me to her lodge. Unfortunately I had no time to take up this offer. Then in Bali, Jayem the course presenter spoke repeatedly about a book he was helping his partner to write. When I returned to Melbourne a few weeks later once again I received a clear inner message to write. I needed to record all my experiences, the dreams and books and songs that I had been guided to. It felt like I was being guided to write a university thesis! Goodness, all I wanted to do was sit on a couch with my legs folded under me, drink a cup of tea with three teaspoons of sugar and eat a slice of cake. Of course none of these were any good for either my varicose veins or my sugar levels. I was fighting a losing battle trying to eliminate sugar from my diet.

I wrote an e-mail to Jayem telling him that I was being guided to write, only I had no idea how to. His prompt reply was, "Write girl. Follow your heart!"

When I mentioned writing to my sons and expressed my doubts they said, "Just do it, Mum."

So I started, terrified. I had no idea where this book would go. The only thing I knew was that it would be called *Desert Wisdom*.

Desert Wisdom is simply asking God, our inner wisdom, before we act. Ask spirit, feel the emotion, use the intellect, then act. It is a bit like the simple rule we use when crossing a road. Stop, look, listen, cross. Easy to remember, sensible to use, ensures our safety and well-being. Similarly, the Desert Wisdom rule helps and assists us in our day to day actions. It is an invitation to our soul to steer this craft, our body. This is the balancing of spirit and matter.

The Aborigine Elders talk of the culture of the mob and their connection to Mother Earth and how much they grieved this separation from Her when they were relocated and dislocated as a result of the colonists' and missionaries' invasion of their land. The colonists and missionaries did not understand the ways of the tribe and imposed their language, their religion, their culture upon a group who lived in Oneness with nature.

The Aborigines had four kanyini that were needed for them to survive, their spirituality, their land, their belief systems and their families. The disintegration of their families as a result of the misguided good intentions of the missionaries, the claiming of their land by power hungry colonists and the disregard of their Gods and belief systems resulted in the annihilation of the structures of the group. The end result—confusion, conflict, deep pain, suffering and alcoholism.

On an individual level we are experiencing this as well. We have forgotten our true essence; our spirituality, we neglect and abuse our bodies and the land, our belief systems have been based on fear and incomplete knowledge and all this has impacted on our families and relationships. The result? Pain, suffering, annihilation, conflict, wars, addictions, confusion and chaos. To heal ourselves, we need to connect to the truth of who we are. When we heal ourselves, we help heal the world.

A few weeks after I returned from Uluru and Bali, I was drawn to an old book that was at the bottom of a drawer. It had been covered by my mother about 20 years ago. It had huge pink roses on it. This turned out to be the third book that Baba had handed to me during the channelling session. In it is the Declaration of the Avatar:

> *'There is no one to know who I am, until I created the Universe at my pleasure with one Word. Immediately, the mountains rose up and rivers started running. The sun, moon and stars sprang from nowhere to prove my existence. Came beasts and birds, flying, speaking, hearing and mankind too. The first place was granted to mankind, and my knowledge was placed in his mind.*

Sri Sathya Sai Baba

About a month after the Uluru trip I was guided to a book called *The Serpent of Light beyond 2012* by Drunvalo Melchizedek. Here he talks about the work he was called to do in 2003, involving the transference of power and responsibility from the male to the female. The ceremony took place on the fourth dimensional plane and he stated that someday this ceremony would take place in the third-dimension to crystallise these energies in our everyday life. The woman to whom the power was transferred immediately flew to a place between the Island of the Sun and the Island of the Moon on Lake Titicaca and planted a crystal deep inside the Earth. Then she flew back out into the atmosphere above the lake and waited. When this second ceremony took place, the female energy would then lead humanity into the light for the next 12,920 years.

After reading this, it felt that when I responded to the call to go to Ayers Rock after the powerful dream and when I stood with the many tourists watching the sun rise on one side and the full moon on the other, I too was part of this ceremony.

Later that month when I was in Bali in the Alam Cinta ashram, Jayem suddenly branched out into an anecdote of something that Jeshua had revealed to him in one of his channelling sessions. He said that many years ago Jeshua had shown him the ley lines on earth and the lines between Uluru and Jerusalem were broken and needed restoring. When he completed the story he said, "Phew, not sure why I had to tell you that, but well I had to . . ." For me this was another message and confirmation. When I answered the call and followed my guidance to go to Uluru it was me listening to spirit. When we listen to spirit, even if we do not fully understand it, we fulfil a part of the divine plan here on earth.

What are you? You are That; you are a spark of the divine. You are not the body, sense, mind, intelligence with which you now identify yourselves. You are God, only caught in deluding yourselves that you are bound by this body.
Sai Baba

Chakras and Energy Vortexes

A FEW WEEKS LATER I was watching a DVD called *Phoenix Rising*, to balance the chakras, and I was breathing deeply and rhythmically. I reasoned that the breathing would open and cleanse the cells while the colour and sound will cleanse and balance my chakras. Then the thought that the Rainbow Serpent I had been contemplating was in fact the chakra system within my body, suddenly flooded my mind. This sunk deep into my cells as a powerful message.

The chakras are inextricably linked with the science and practice of yoga. Yoga is a system of philosophy and practice designed to connect the body to its divine nature of pure consciousness. The origin of yoga and the earliest mention of chakras go back to the Vedas. In addition, Tantric teachings which became popular in the sixth and seventh century A.D, denotes the chakra system as the weaving of polarities of spirit and matter, mind and body, masculine and feminine and Heaven and Earth.

The chakras in the human body are vortexes of energy and light in the colours of the rainbow. When our energy bodies are balanced we help balance the energies of Mother Earth. To do this we need to cleanse our bodies, minds and souls. The body is a vehicle of consciousness. Chakras are the wheels of life that carry this vehicle about—through its trials, tribulations and transformations. When we understand the purpose of each chakra system and we bring it into harmony we become receptive to the divine universe. This is not only beneficial for our well-being but also a way of uniting the Individual Soul with the Universal Soul.

The chakras exist within the subtle body, interpenetrating the physical body. The subtle body is the non-physical psychic body that is superimposed on our physical bodies. It can be measured as electromagnetic force fields within and around all living creatures. The chakras are the psychic generators of the auric fields. The aura itself is the meeting point between the core patterns generated by the chakras and the influence of the external world.

I do not attempt to explain the chakra system in depth here because there are many wonderful books available and there are many others who have a greater more in-depth knowledge in this field. What I do know is that just as it is necessary for us to maintain and care for our physical bodies, it is vital for us to maintain our energetic bodies as well.

There are many ways of balancing the chakras, for example, visualisations, deep breathing, colour therapy, exercises and pranic healing. Balancing the chakras must become a part of our daily routine. Just as we brush our teeth and shower without giving these a second thought, so too must the care of our energetic bodies become second nature.

Sai Baba made His presence known to me twice in this teaching. One day, while at a Brahma Kumaris meditation retreat, a lady told me about a kinesiologist that she was seeing and she suggested that I consult him too. She then took a card out of her bag and handed it to me. Since she was someone I had only just met a few minutes prior, I found her promptings a bit strange. However, a few weeks later I was at home and was feeling weak and exhausted. I was not physically ill but felt depleted of energy. Just then the phone rang. It was Paula. She said that she was thinking of me and asked if I had made an appointment with the kinesiologist. When I ended the conversation I decided that I would make that call and set up an appointment. A week later I lay on the narrow blue medical bed in Dale Anderson's consulting room as he worked on me. His hands hovered above my body and I could feel waves and circles of energy moving within my body. When the consultation was over and Dale and I chatted, I glanced above his head at the bookshelf and there staring back at me was a photograph of a smiling Sai Baba.

This happened once again at a health retreat in Bali in January 2010. A cranio–sacral therapist, an American woman whose name happened to be Paula as well, was treating me when I suddenly felt the strong presence of Sai Baba. I shot into an upright position and I asked her if she knew Baba. She then looked deep into my eyes, got up and handed me the little photograph she had on her shelf. Quite cryptically she then said, "So you are the one I was waiting for. You are the reason Baba appeared to me again." She was a lady of few words. Paula had a reputation in the retreat for being bad-tempered, rude and abrupt.Once again I cried at the strength and mystery of Baba's love. When I attempted to return the Sai photograph she told me to keep it.

I was being taught to come back to explore the sacred architecture of the body and the psyche. When all the chakras are understood, opened and connected, we have then bridged the gulf between matter and spirit, understanding that we are the rainbows that connect earth and heaven. This was a reminder once again to return to the self.

The result of having a balanced energetic system is a higher level of consciousness. When a person evolves to a higher level of consciousness, he or she will be incapable of inflicting harm, for the soul's new vibrational frequency will carry an agenda that no longer supports the lower behaviours.

A book on the chakra system, *The Wheels of Life* by Anodea Judith, was one of the first books I was guided to, though like a child learning to play a new musical instrument my practice has been erratic. However, I have had many reminders and promptings to keep at it, so I have become better. Now balancing my chakras is something I do every morning and night.

Thoughts, words and deeds must be in harmony.
Sai Baba

The Lord Returns

Just before the beginning of the current age in which we are living, known in the East as the Kali or Iron Age, the sage Markandeya recorded a conversation he had with God Vishnu, the embodiment of the preserver aspect of the trinity. In a passage in the Mahabharata text, it is recorded that Vishnu spoke of a time during the darkest period of the Kali Age when human values would deteriorate, violence and injustice would be widespread, falsehood would triumph over truth, oppression and crime would be prevalent. Vishnu told how he would take a human birth in order to intervene and set the world on a new course.

Here is the text of that statement.

> When evil is rampant upon this earth, I will take birth
> in the family of a virtuous man, and assume a human body
> to restore tranquillity by the extermination of all evils. For
> the preservation of rectitude and morality, I will assume
> an inconceivable human form when the season for action
> comes. In the Kali Age of sin I will assume an Avatar
> form that is dark in colour. I will be born in a family in
> south India. This Avatar will possess great energy, great
> intelligence and great powers. Material objects needed
> for this Avatar's mission will be at his disposal as soon
> as He will think of them. He will be victorious with the
> strength of virtue. He will restore order and peace in the

world. This Avatar will inaugurate a new era of truth, and will be surrounded by spiritual people. He will roam over the earth adored by the spiritual people. The people of the earth will imitate this Avatar's conduct, and there will be prosperity and peace. Men will once more betake themselves to the practice of religious rites. Educational centres, for the cultivation of Brahmic lore and temples will reappear again everywhere. Ashrams will be filled with men of truth. Rulers of the earth will govern their kingdoms virtuously. The Avatar will have an illustrious reputation.

The Avatar mentioned in this text is referred to as the Kalki Avatar. The advent of this Avatar has been known of and predicted for thousands of years in various holy books and obscure texts including the Book of Revelations, Nostradamus, The Ocean of Light, an ancient Persian manuscript of the revelations of Prophet Mohammed, and the Shuka Naadi Granthi—containing detailed prophecies of the Kalki Avatar written on hundreds of palm leaf manuscripts by Sage Shuka over 5000 years ago. The time of great evil mentioned in the prophecies corresponds to the Twentieth Century with its World Wars, regimes of mad dictators and authoritarian rulers, nuclear weapons, famines, diseases, pollution, crime, violence, catastrophes, and worldwide decline of morality.

Baba says:

No one can understand my Mystery. The best you can do is to get immersed in it. It is no use you arguing about pros and cons; dive and know the depth; eat and know the taste. You must dive deep into the sea to get the pearls. What good is it to dabble among the waves near the shore, and swear that the sea has no pearls in it and that all tales about them are false? So also if you must realise the full fruit of this Avathar, dive deep and get immersed in Sai Baba. Half-heartedness, hesitation, doubt, cynicism,

*listening to tales, all is of no avail. Concentrated complete
faith—that alone can bring victory.*

*In truth you cannot understand the nature of My
Reality, either today, or even after a thousand years of
steady austerity or ardent inquiry, even if all mankind
joins in that effort. But, in a short time, you will become
cognizant of the Bliss showered by the Divine Principle
which has taken upon itself this sacred body and this
sacred Name. Your good fortune, which will provide you
this chance, is greater than that which was available for
anchorites, monks, sages, saints, and even personalities
embodying facets of Divine Glory. Do not allow doubt to
distract you; if only you will install in the altar of your
heart steady faith in My Divinity, you can win a vision
of My Reality.*

When Krishna lived on the Earth, few were aware of his divinity
although he successfully accomplished his mission of ridding the
earth of many powerful and evil personalities. Shirdi Sai Baba was an
incarnation of God Shiva but most regarded him as a very great saint.
Only a few of his closest devotees knew him to be an incarnation. It
is difficult to grasp the implications of the Divine in human form. If
we accept the Advaitha philosophy that there is One only without a
second; nothing but God throughout the manifested universe and
beyond, then logically we are in God, God is in us, we are God. The
Atma within us—our innermost awareness is the Eternal Witness,
a spark of the Eternal Flame. God enjoys the play of this universe by
sporting inside the various manifested forms as the Atmic awareness
of each. All this apparent diversity is only the illusion of Maya—the
formless taking on form, the Eternal manifesting in time and space
and then indwelling each form as the Atmic spark within. Thus He
sees all, knows all, and is all. Really the form of the Avatar is like a
focal point wherein this colossal Divine force can contact the human
in the tiny knot of energy that is our Earth, on the fleeting time scale
that is a human lifetime. But the Avatar is in no way limited by the
constriction of bodily confinement because He is one with the source
of all.

Baba says:

> *The Avatar takes the human form and behaves in a human way so that humanity can feel kinship with the divinity. At the same time he rises to godly heights so that mankind also can aspire to reach God.*
>
> *People could not stand the Lord in super-human form. If the Lord came in all His majesty people would be afraid and would have no opportunity to know and love him. It is only when the Lord comes in a human body that people are able to approach him and learn to love him and know him even a little bit. But one should not make the mistake of thinking that is all there is. For instance, the airplane flying high in the sky descends to the airport. But one should not make the mistake of thinking that the plane is a ground machine because they see it on the ground. In like fashion, although the Lord has made a landing here on earth, so to speak, He is not limited to His human form.*
>
> *I am new and ever ancient. I come always for the restoration of Dharma (righteousness), for tending the virtuous and ensuring those conditions congenial for progress, and for educating the "blind" who miss the way and wander into the wilderness. Some doubters might ask, can Parabrahman assume human form? Well, man can derive joy only through the human frame; he can receive instruction, inspiration, illumination only through human language and human communication.*
>
> *The Avatar appears to be human and we are misled into thinking of him in these terms but the Avatar himself warns us against this error.*

Sathya Sai Baba once responded to a devotee who asked when he should return for another visit: *"First understand that you do not need to come back to see this little body,"* he said pointing to himself. Then he added, *"Find me in your heart."*

In his previous embodiment as Shirdi Sai Baba (1835-1918) he made a similar statement to his devotees:

"Though, I am here bodily, still I know what you do; beyond the seven seas. Go wherever you will, over the wide world, I am with you. My abode is in your heart and I am within you. Always worship Me, Who is seated in your heart, as well as in the hearts of all beings." Shirdi Sai Baba

Sathya Sai Baba, who is the second incarnation of Shirdi Sai Baba, echoes this thought in many of his statements:

You may be seeing me today for the first time, but you are all old acquaintances for Me. I know you through and through. My task is the spiritual regeneration of Humanity through Truth and Love. If you approach one step nearer to me, I shall advance three steps towards you.

Wherever you walk, I am there. Whomsoever you contact, I am in that person. I am in each. From each, I will respond. You can see Me in one place and miss Me in another. You cannot escape Me or do anything in secret.

In past ages, when the power of evil reached a certain stage, the Divine descended into form to suppress the evil and to foster the good. In the Kali age in which we are living, evil has reached new depths. Of all the various ages—each with its own characteristics, the Kali age is the age of the deepest descent into matter and form, away from spirit. We have passed through the lowest point of the pendulum, the dark times of this 20th century and are now beginning the upward climb. The appearance of the Avatar coincides with the darkest hour of the Kali Yuga.

Baba says:

People tell me that mankind is on the brink of destruction, that the forces of hypocrisy and hate are fast prevailing on all continents, and that anxiety and fear are stalking the streets of every city and village in the world; there is no need to tell me this, for I have come precisely

for this reason. When the world is on the verge of chaos, the Avatar comes to still the storm raging in the hearts of men. Prasanthi, the higher Peace, will be established soon; the demonic deviations from the straight Divine Path will be corrected. Dharma will be revived and re-vitalised in every human community.

God incarnates for the revival of Dharma (Righteousness) which includes morality, truth, virtue, love and a host of other qualities that uphold the communities of man as well as the individual. The other purposes usually given—serving the devoted, destroying the wicked, re-establishing the sacred tradition—these are all secondary. For, he who is righteous will be guarded from harm, by righteousness itself; he who is unrighteous will fall into disaster through the evil that he perpetrates. The one task includes all else.

For the protection of the virtuous, for the destruction of evil-doers and for establishing righteousness on a firm footing, I incarnate from age to age. Whenever asanthi, or disharmony, overwhelms the world, the Lord will incarnate in human form to establish the modes of earning prasanthi, or peace, and to re-educate the human community in the paths of peace.

The Avatar comes to transform humanity but this must take place through the transformation of individuals making up humanity. To raise bread we mix a pinch of yeast into the dough and the action of the yeast spreads throughout the mix, eventually leavening the entire loaf. So the Avatar works through individuals, transforming them into the divine beings they essentially are. The light from the many individuals gradually dispels the darkness of ignorance, impacting all of humanity.

Through interviews with devotees who come to see Him, Sai Baba reveals that He knows intimate details of their lives including physical problems and issues dominating their lives, sometimes even events they themselves have long forgotten. Though Baba left school at the age of fourteen saying, "My devotees are calling me," he has been known to speak to people from all over the world using words from their own language. Though Baba never read the Indian classics he liberally sprinkles appropriate stories from them in his talks. Baba quotes long passages in the ancient mother language Sanskrit, and assists Brahmic priests in correctly carrying out elaborate Vedic rituals. He tells of undocumented events and conversations in the lives of sages, holy persons, and historic persons as if he were there at the time of their happening. To all who come to him he makes them feel as if he were their own. He constantly exudes bliss and love and all who come to him regard him as they would a loving parent.

Sai Baba never appears rushed or hurried and yet he accomplishes more than ten or even a hundred humans ever could. He is in constant motion from early morning until night greeting visitors, going over plans, giving darshan and interviews, taking letters, attending bhajans and taking part in and planning ceremonial events. He dedicates his entire life to his devotees and his mission with absolutely no attachment to possessions, personal time, or ordinary human pursuits.

Baba says:

> *My work is ceaseless and so your work, too, is without end. Know that I am within you and without you. There is no difference. Rid yourselves of petty matters for ever more. You are now ME and I am now THEE. There is no difference. My Darshan will pour forth from ME to and through you. You may be unaware of this constant action. Be ever pure in heart and soul, and mankind in your lifetime will benefit from your unique qualities.*
>
> *This is a great chance. Be confident that you will all be liberated. Know that you are saved. Many hesitate to believe that things will improve, that life will be happy for all and full of joy, and that the golden age will recur. Let me assure you that this dharmaswarupa, that this divine body, has not come in vain. It will succeed in averting the crisis that has come upon humanity.*

In my present Avatar, I have come armed with the fullness of the power of formless God to correct mankind, raise human consciousness and put people back on the right path of truth, righteousness, peace and love to divinity.

In this avathar [Divine Incarnation], the wicked will not be destroyed; they will be corrected and reformed and educated and led back to the path from which they have strayed.

We have a unique opportunity to take part in the transformation of our planet during this time of great change. We must start by transforming ourselves.

Baba says:

I have come to give you the key to the treasure of ananda, or bliss, to teach you how to tap that spring, for you have forgotten the way to blessedness. If you waste this time of saving yourselves, it is just your fate. You have come to get from me tinsel and trash, the petty little cures and promotions, worldly joys and comforts. Very few of you desire to get from me the thing that I have come to give you: namely, liberation itself. Even among these few, those who stick to the path of sadhana, or spiritual practice, and succeed are a handful.

I am determined to correct you only after informing you of my credentials. That is why I am now and then announcing my Nature by means of miracles, that is, acts which are beyond human capacity and human understanding. Not that I am anxious to show off my Powers. The object is to draw you closer to me, to cement your hearts to me.

I ask only that you turn to me when your mind drags you into grief or pride or envy. Bring me the depths of your mind, no matter how grotesque, how cruelly ravaged by doubts or disappointments. I know how to treat them. I will not reject you. I am your mother.

Why fear when I am here? Put all your faith in Me. I shall guide and guard you.

The godliness which is present in everybody in the form of a little spark exists in me as the full flame, and it is my mission to develop every little spark of God in everyone to the fullness of the divine flame.

Where there is a desire for mental tranquillity, I hurry to grant tranquillity. Where there is dispiritedness, I hasten to raise the drooping heart. Where there is no mental trust, I rush to restore trust. I am ever on the move to fulfil the mission for which I have come.

I never utter a word that does not have significance, or do a deed without beneficial consequence.

What I will, must take place; what I plan must succeed. Transformation must begin with the individual. For when the individual changes, the world will change too. This transformation has to take place in the minds of men. Right thoughts will lead to right actions.

Do not bother about what has happened in the past. Get immersed in the tasks of the present. Render service with a pure and selfless heart. The delight of the individual gladdens the Divine. Equally the Divine esteems you. Do everything with the Lord's name on your lips. Develop all that is good in you and share that goodness with one and all.

Everything points to the terror of conflagration coming; and my mission is to pre-empt the fires by re-establishing dharma and the spiritual law of one God, one religion, one language [of the heart] embracing one humanity . . . . I want to build one humanity without any religious, caste or other barriers in a universal empire of love which could enable my devotees to feel the whole world as their family.

If God Himself is here to foster Dharma, and you engage yourself in the same task, then you are worshiping Him. Then you are near and dear to Him, for you are serving Him, His devotees, and yourself.

My Mission has now reached that point in time when each one of you now has work to do. This planet has a purpose in the great galaxy in which it is held. That purpose is now unfolding before your eyes. I call upon you to radiate the Devotion within you so that its unseen power will envelop all who come into your orbit. To successfully perform your part, always remain centred upon me. Allow yourself to impart that purity of heart within you towards all human beings and all living creatures and do not reach for the fruits of your work. This part of My Mission is performed in absolute silence. You are My instruments from whom My love will pour. Be always aware that the moment you let your ego descend upon you, My work ceases. When you have overcome your negative unmindfulness you will again become My source. The multiplication of My Love will be felt throughout the world. I have drawn you to Me. I have made great steps in My Mission over these past Incarnations.

So, in your lives, by your examples, live and practise My message, knowing that some will understand and others will not. Have no concern with the outcome of your efforts, for some people are ready and others are not. Each one is free to go his own way in his own time. Many will choose to remain in darkness with all the attachments that hold them back from the true path. But, eventually, their time will come and, one day, all will be re-united in the Kingdom of God.

The seeds are in the ground, germinating, as the teachings of the Lord begins to spread throughout the world and infiltrates the minds of men. What will emerge will brighten the world as the beauty of the absolute truths, that 'I and My Father are One', and 'Only Love is Real', begin to reach millions. It is a process that takes time and the new Golden Age will evolve gradually.

Our responsibility is to serve this process. We must let the divinity that is within each and every one of us, shine forth and thereby become one of the great beacons to light up the world and hasten the arrival of the new Golden Age.

As Anne Lamott states; "Lighthouses don't go running all over an island looking for ships to save, they just stand there shining."

When we choose love and happiness, we choose to live from our authentic selves, which is the voice of God. When we choose to love all and serve all from a pure heart we serve the divine plan here on earth.

You should know that you are born to achieve great and stupendous tasks in life. You are the children of God; heroes in action, great soldiers in the age of Kali, full of compassion and Divine love and resolved to make Divinity resound with success in the world.
Sai Baba

Bringing Lucifer off the shelf

I WAS GUIDED TO MANY books and many songs. I would have dreams, experiences and thoughts then would be guided to a book where I would read passages that were related directly to these. Some songs that I had heard many times before suddenly felt like direct messages to me. If I ignored a book it would come up over and over again until I took notice. I had no idea what was happening, I could not explain it.

One night I had an experience where I felt a presence next to my bed and felt or heard someone say to me, "You are the Goddess Lakshmi." I, of-course, dismissed this immediately as my imagination and said aloud how ludicrous that was. As far as I was concerned, Lakshmi was the Goddess you prayed to. However, the next day I received a picture of the Goddess in the mail. This too, I dismissed as mere co-incidence. The following day, I went along to a meditation with Selvie and Reuben, my cousin and her husband. After the meditation, while browsing through the small bookshop, I picked up a book called; *The perfect relationship: The guru and his student.* Out of this book fell two photographs. I stooped to pick them up. They were of the Goddess Lakshmi. The bookseller gasped, because she had lost these photographs two years earlier and had been looking for them ever since. I told her that I thought it was a sign for me to buy one. I could not ignore this anymore. She replied that they were not for sale because she had not priced them, but as I was about to leave the shop she changed her mind and said, "You're right, it is for you." I purchased the picture of Lakshmi for $20 and left the shop knowing deeply that this was no co-incidence.

Some of the books were easier to accept than others. When I was guided to *Tantra:The path to ecstasy*, I had a serious talk with the man above. What was He thinking!!! As far as I was concerned Tantra meant sex and orgies. I read this book like a teenager with a pornographic magazine. I would take it out late at night when my 16 year old son was in bed, and then I would use another book to cover the title. I couldn't have him thinking that his 44 year old mother had left his father and was now looking for exciting sex! The Gods must surely have been laughing hysterically at this whole drama.

Tantra is both a science and a spiritual path. As a spiritual path it emphasizes purification of the mind and heart and the cultivation of a spiritually illuminating philosophy of life. As a science, it experiments with techniques whose effectiveness depends on the precise application of mantra and yantra, ritual use, performance of tantric mudras and accompanying mental exercises. Accomplished tantrics see the world and everything in it as an indivisible whole—as a tangible manifestation of the Divine Mother. This is not a metaphor for them, nor a philosophical premise; it is a living breathing reality. Where most see duality—young and old, right and wrong, male and female, pure and impure—a tantric adept sees One. The Divine Mother is not in the world; she is the world. Indeed She is the universe, and to see any difference between the individual self and Her or between Her and any natural force or cosmic influence is misperception. The misconception we have of ourselves consists in looking upon ourselves as ego—personalities rather than the indivisible pure Being-Consciousness.

Another time there was melodrama was when I was guided to a book on Lucifer. I was walking along Swanston Street in Melbourne when I spotted a book on Lucifer in a second hand bookstore. I had no desire to read a book on the fallen angel but I was drawn to this one. I tried walking away but just could not. It felt like some invisible force was holding me there. So I stood on the sidewalk and prayed to Sai Baba. I did not want to be led to the dark side and something was compelling me to read this book. I walked reluctantly into the shop, lowered my voice to barely above a whisper and asked if I could have a look at that book. I could not bring myself to say the word. The book was on display in the store front and needed to be brought down with a ladder. The salesman then turned to his assistant who was, as fate would have it, at the other end of the store and yelled out to him to bring the ladder over and get Lucifer off the shelf!!!

I was mortified. I thought that all the customers in the shop were looking at me and thinking, "Here stands a Satan follower." The urge to flee was overpowering—then the book was in my hand. I opened to a random page and the first thing I read was, *"Lucifer— who is emphatically not the Evil One, but the spirit of human progress, the fight to learn and grow, to be independent and proud, but also spiritually free. Lucifer simply means 'the light bringer', the enlightener. The intellectual Lucifer is the spirit of intelligence and love; it is the Paraclete, it is the Holy Spirit, while the physical Lucifer is the great agent of universal magnetism. Lucifer, the Morning Star is all brightness and hope especially during the times we are in."*

Phew, I could breathe again. So I bought the book, this time with my head held up and walked out. But not before looking around the shop and noticing that no-one was the least bit interested in what I was doing or buying. It had all been my imagination.

I wished the books I was guided to were easy reads, but that was not to be. Most followed the standard set by *A Course in Miracles*. So I had to read, then re-read sections to understand what I had read. If I was not concentrating fully I would miss the entire meaning then have to go back several pages. I started to sense energy from the very words itself. I could feel what was written with divine guidance and parts of the book that seemed to be the author's mind.

When I was guided much later to the book, *Opening to Channel* by Sanaya Roman and Duane Packer I learnt that our guides have many ways of reaching us. Often messages are sent through books, songs, rainbows, people, teachers, words in conversation—things that speak directly to your heart.

My personal journey was that I had the experience first and then it was explained through any one of the above. My guides seemed to be using all channels to get to me.

My sister often asked me, "What do you mean guided? We all read books." I can not answer this question with any degree of logic. I can say that when I was being directed to a new book, my body would vibrate, I would have a deep sense of knowing and the words would suddenly catch my attention. If I ignored it, it would turn up again and again. At times it felt like the Big Guy had a stack of books under His arm and was handing them out to me as soon as I was done with the previous one. I was getting a new education. Distant learning had taken on a new meaning.

The mere reading of a book or journal will not bring about discrimination. That which is seen, heard or read about, must be put into actual practice. Without this, reading is a mere waste of time.
Sai Baba

Trance States

I WAS AT A STAFF meeting in school when the principal announced, "Today is the last day to put in your request for leave for 2010." I had not consciously thought about taking leave but suddenly I knew I must. I checked with our business manager to see if I had accumulated enough leave and she confirmed that I did. Within a few days my leave form was submitted and the leave was granted.

Six months later I started the long service leave. I had a term off school. The day before the leave started I wondered what I would do with myself for three whole months. I had no travel plans and certainly no planned agenda. However, I quite liked the idea of hovering around my sons like other stay at home mums, providing fresh home cooked meals and a listening ear when it was required. But the divine had other plans for me.

When I awoke the next morning, I felt that my whole being seemed to be preparing for something. I drove my son Deshlin to school and got back home by 8.30am. A few minutes after entering the house I was overcome by a strange sense of drowsiness. I had no option but to lie down again. Then I started to have a series of dreams. I call these dreams here because that is what I thought they were. I was, however, half awake during these episodes. It seemed like I was going to the movies! After a while, I would get up and record pages of information in my dream journal. This went on for a few weeks. Does God keep time? I don't know. But somebody seemed to know when it was a convenient time for me.

Later I understood that some of what I experienced were trance states. If I knew that I was going into a trance state I would have baulked at the idea. The word trance conjured up images of men and women with strange white markings across their faces and chests and needles pierced grotesquely through their tongues and flesh.

When I was little my family took annual trips to a temple in Isipingo, Durban, to attend a special Easter prayer festival. I loved these trips. My mother would have the day off work, which was rare for her and the entire family would board the train to the temple. Now to a Londoner or Melbournian taking a train in the 70's was nothing out of the ordinary, but to the average Indian family living in South Africa it was like getting onto the space shuttle Columbia and going to the moon. At the railway station, my mother would buy each of us a pop-a-2 or a three-coloured umbrella ice-cream. The ice-cream cart was a little ice-box attached to the front of a bicycle and the ice-cream man would ring a hand-held bell announcing his presence. Armed with ice-creams and large grins the three girls dressed in their Sunday bests, would clamber onto the train and rush for a window seat. Then there was a lot of seat hopping, loud talking, sticky fingers and dripping ice-creams and soon my best dress would transform itself into a polka frock.

Hundreds of people attended these Easter prayer events. Women cooked sweet rice or biryanis over wood fires and offered this food (Prasad) to anyone who would accept it. In addition to this endless supply of free food, there were food-stalls that sold fizzy drinks, fruit, toys and miscellaneous prayer items. It was like going to the fun-fare. My sisters and I would wander from stall to stall and gathering to gathering while my mother and Ayah, my grandmother, cooked and prepared for the prayer and my father rested under a shady tree.

During these Easter festivals people would take religious vows. Essentially they made deals with the Gods and promised to perform a sacrifice if their prayers were answered. Some sacrificed chickens and this was cooked on outdoor fires and offered to all those present. As the years passed I noticed that chickens were no longer sacrificed but rather used as prayer tools. The priest would grip the poor helpless chicken tightly in his hand, and then swing it thrice around the head of the person who had taken the vow. The chicken would then be thrown onto the roof of the temple. The prayer was done. Often as we walked around the temple I would observe a temple worker bring these chickens down stealthily and then they would reappear at the entrance of the temple ready for resale! Recycled chickens? Or was it the cycle of life?

Ayah, my grandmother was convinced that someone had cast an evil eye on me because I was very thin and ate very little. The fact that I had boundless amounts of energy and represented my school in numerous athletic events had no effect on her. This is what her deal with the Gods must surely have sounded like.

"Dear God, please fatten Vasi up. In return, I promise that I will get her to strip down to her underwear in the presence of the hundreds of people in the temple. I will then get her to wear a garland of 'sling-a-berry' leaves around her waist which will leave no room for modesty. I will listen to none of her protests. Thank you God."

My first experience of people in trance states was at these events. According to my mother, they would fast and pray for many days, reach these altered states and were then able to walk on hot coals or get their bodies pierced. The men and women had thick, long needles pierced through their tongues and these hung hideously out of their mouths. Sharp menacing—looking hooks hung off their backs and sometimes things were attached to these hooks. It all looked very painful and I could not understand much of it at all. It was all a rather frightful sight.

I would stand well away from it all and watch from the safety of my mother's back. The people in these trance states would follow a special chariot which was adorned with idols and garlands. The spectators, the temple goers, would follow closely and watch in awe, curiosity and devotion. People would throw coins, flowers and little copper idols onto these carriages and the children would help themselves to the coins that fell onto the ground.

With the exception of the people in these trance states and the humiliation of having to walk around the temple nearly naked, the annual trips were ones of great enjoyment and merriment. Prayer and God were very far from my mind.

My trance-like states, if that was what they were, came upon me without me actually doing anything. Were these connections with God, spirit, my higher Self? I'm not sure. I just know that they happened and it seemed to be for my healing and for my learning.

Anyone who is engaged in prayer, worship and discipline, and who has self-control, faith, patience, kindness, joy and pure love towards me, (who is present in all) is precious to me.
Sai Baba

Know Thyself Know God

I WAS ALSO GUIDED TO listen to a section of the Bhagavad Gita, called the 'Krishna-Arjuna dialogue. The dialogue is an adaptation from the original text and was inspired by Sai Baba's teaching. Baba says that whenever Mahatma Ghandhi felt disillusioned he would read this chapter. The recording was a simplified English version. I would have made no sense of the comprehensive version. Here my Guru, was being compassionate, I think. However, even the children's version of the Gita is pretty difficult to absorb. I understood poor Arjuna's dilemma completely. I had all the same questions, the same doubts and same fears. Lord Krishna's advice to Arjuna applies to all in every age because life is often a battle against all kinds of odds. This knowledge imparted by Lord Krishna is timeless; it is called atmanayga, the knowledge of the Self.

Chapter 2 of the Gita is called the sankia yoga, meaning the path of wisdom. Lord Krishna reminds Arjuna that we are not this body but the atma, the soul wearing a dress called the body. This is referred to as the jivatma. Jiva means life or living object. So jivatma means life within the cocoon called the body and the mind. The jivatma is like an actor wearing a particular dress on this stage called life and we are all playing different roles in the cosmic drama scripted, directed and produced by God.

In a play, the actor is given a part that he must act out. It is his free choice how he acts out these parts. This is individual freedom. The entire play is impacted by his actions. For the play to be successful all actors must perform their parts effectively.

In the drama of life, speaking proper dialogue means following one's natural dharma or following one's heart, the spiritual heart, the atma which is the indweller, the divine resident, God within.

When we think we are the body, feelings of mine arise and these result in body consciousness, and the dream of separation. We are not the perishable body. We are all the eternal atma, so we cannot die. The atma shines as the consciousness and the resident of the heart. This heart refers to the spiritual heart and not the physical heart. This divine resident is sometimes called the indweller or simply as God. So as God resides within you, you do not have to look for him outside of you, just within.

The resident in the heart is love itself. Since God is in all, when I love, it is me loving God and when I am loved it is God loving me. The very love we feel for the things we do, right here on earth, is us loving as God loves. For all things is God. To love what we do and do what we love, that is divine. So loving to live and living to love, is the love of God being expressed in this world.

When we listen to our hearts and act according to this inner voice we are in fact fulfilling our purpose here on earth. In this way we bring peace to earth and harmony and love prevails. For when we are happy and peaceful with our choices, all benefit. We have free will, our mind quietens and we feel a sense of peace and harmony deep within. We are living in love, which is a connection to our divine self.

Fear however often obscures the truth of love. Feelings of guilt, anxiety, rejection, exclusion, anger, lack of clarity, perceived unfairness, being told how to think and being judged, are things that send us into the danger zone of fear.

Where there is fear, there is discord and disharmony. This results in a lower frequency and therefore a lower consciousness.

Often fear operates so insidiously in our lives that we are not aware of it. When fear cloaks itself as love it is very hard to detect. Our responsibility to self is to look for that fear. Contemplate. Inquire within. Often they stem from belief and value systems that no longer hold true for you.

Jeshua, in his teachings called *Way of the Heart* as channelled by Jayem, says, ". . . *cultivate within you the decision to turn your attention upon your own mind, upon your own behaviour, upon what is true and real for you, moment by moment—to study it, to consider it, to feel it, to breathe the Light of Spirit through it, and to constantly retrain the mind so that it assumes complete responsibility in each moment."*

We need to make the decision to live in love, joy, peace, happiness and kindness. We need the intellect for this decision; this is conscious choice and individual freedom. For in reality there are no flaws, there is only perfection. That perfection is you, is us—God's perfect creation.

When you learn to focus on your relationship with the self and become authentic listeners to your own inner wisdom you realise that there is no one to blame outside of you.

When I started to practise these exercises I often felt I was stuck inside the movie *Ground Hog's Day*, a movie where the protagonist wakes up each day and finds that he is exactly where he was the day before. I observed events and dramas replaying it-self over and over again. Ones I had blamed others for and had all the evidence and reasons to be justified came up again and again. It was only when I learnt to observe them curiously and deliberately chose to react differently that they seemed to dissolve miraculously from my field of awareness. I started to see co-incidences all around me. I now know that there are no co-incidences. All occurs for our learning.

I often imagine my life as one of those interactive computer games my son loves so much. I am both a character within the game being controlled by an outside force, the supreme Father but I am also the controller of the character which I have chosen and created. So I am both the created and the creator in this game called Life.

The world is nothing but reaction, reflection and resound. Whatever you do will come back to you, and nothing else. This is Divine Law.
Sai Baba

Baba teaches me through worms

Two worms' related anecdotes helped me understand my lessons and experiences further. The first I read in a book called *Shri Sai Satcharita* on the life and teachings of Shirdhi Sai Baba, the first incarnation of Sri Sathya Sai Baba.

A certain Dr Pillay had a swollen leg and was experiencing excruciating pain. He had tried many different remedies to no avail. All he wanted then was release from this torture. He prayed to Shirdhi Baba to allow him to die. Baba instructed that Dr Pillay be carried to the ashram, and he was told that it was not his time to die as yet. Baba ordered him to sit beside Him and then informed Dr Pillay that a crow would peck his leg and this would cure him. So he sat on the floor of the ashram, next to Baba, with his red, swollen throbbing leg stretched out in front of him. At the same time, a devotee was bent over his task of sweeping the ashram floor. When he came close to Dr Pillay, he did not notice the outstretched leg and he accidentally kicked and tripped over it. Dr Pillay screamed out in agony as the tight swollen red skin burst open and seven guinea worms popped out of the leg.

At first, the pain was so intense, so unbearably agonising that he could hardly cope with it. However, soon his cries fluctuated between pain and moments of relief. Then the periods of relief were more than the periods of pain. Shirdi Baba then told him to rest for 10 days and he would be healed completely. He was.

This story affected me deeply. The thought of worms under the skin repulsed and horrified me. The images of worms exploding from the leg played incessantly in my mind for days. I knew that I was being prompted to contemplate this story deeply.

Then it came to me that the pain of the swollen leg was the pain I had been feeling over the last few years. I too had tried every thing I knew and was at the end of my tether. The 'kick' of my husband's betrayal, the broken marriage and eventual divorce revealed the worms that had been causing me so much pain but which I was blind to. The worms were my belief systems, fears, childhood experiences, harmful relationships, low self esteem, misguided religious teachings, and my own perceptions and thinking.

Immediately this realisation was made, it felt like my psychic teacher said, "Oh yes she's got that, now we can move on." That afternoon another worm story was sent to me, this time via D'Avery's girlfriend. Her 96year old grandfather had a large skin cancer on his leg. An operation was risky at his age and he was sent home and told that it would be monitored. The next time he visited the doctor it was discovered that the cancer was cured because maggots had gotten into the infection and had eaten up the cancer.

The worms that caused the pain were also the ones that cured the disease. They are neither good nor bad. Both are the grace of God, sent as healing or learning for us. Of—course more often than not when we are going through periods of intense pain it is hard to see it as God's love. We yell angrily at God for punishing us. Our emotions fluctuate from anger, to despair, to hope, to grief, to sadness and the list goes on. Well, mine certainly did.

Can we, or should we be stopping these emotions? No, I don't believe so. Our emotions are our inbuilt alarms. We need to see it, feel it, and experience it. We should not try to suppress them but rather observe them as passing clouds. Some clouds are a little darker and stay a little longer and others pass swiftly. Our mind must help us remember our divinity even as we observe the passing showers.

Jayem, as part of the Way of Mastery teachings, uses a process called Radical Inquiry that is very useful to help one get to the source of one's emotions and faulty belief systems. Brandon Bay uses questions as a means to lower ourselves into source, our true self. The Vedanta instructs that we use questions to inquire and contemplate and Socrates taught the same thing to his students.

Man needs to use his mind to contemplate deeply. Our awareness of our thoughts is our responsibility. As Sai Baba says, "How the mind functions and how it issues commands should be well understood by man, only then will he be able to utilise the infinite energy within himself for good." Positive thinking, based on identifying beliefs and assumptions that no longer serve us, can elicit the best from man and help him to use all his energy for his improvement. The improvement of man means the improvement of families, the improvement of families mean the improvement of communities, nations, and the world.

In the poem *Homecoming,* the Australian poet Bruce Dawe refers to the effects of death as the 'spider-web of grief'. This metaphor suggests the connectedness of all people in times of sadness and illustrates the widespread effects of death. In the same way, our good thoughts (sankalpas) affect all in a ripple effect. Each individual is a matrix point in the web of life and each has the responsibility at his or her point on the grid. So developing an awareness of our own thoughts, is not only beneficial for us, but is a necessary service for all of mankind.

Negative thinking stems from fear and fear is formed by ignorance and imagination. In South Africa, when Nelson Mandela became president, while this was a momentous occasion, the predominant feeling among many South Africans was one of fear. Fear of the unknown, fear of the new. Many, like me, left the country with our families at a time when the levels of crimes had increased dramatically, with many of us having been affected directly. In times of transition, chaos often reigns. This is necessary to herald in the new.

Similarly, we are now in a life changing moment. The energies of the earth are transforming and we are moving into another dimension of existence. A new existence is being birthed. Once again, we are being faced with an unknown, only this time, leaving does not seem to be an option. To assist the birthing of the new, we need to overcome this fear of the unknown and trust a higher wisdom. The Higher Wisdom is your own inner being. To trust a higher wisdom, we need to develop awareness—awareness of the self and of the present moment.

Once we see all of our life as learning experiences we realise that there are no failures. All are lessons that we have chosen to experience in this school called our life. And who is the 'we' but a spark of That One, we call God.

The first spiritual discipline is to search for the faults and weaknesses within yourself and to strive to correct them and become perfect.
Sai Baba

My journey continues in Bali
—The Way of Mastery

I CAME ACROSS THE PALPABLE Forgiveness course when I was researching sacred sites after I had the Rainbow Serpent Dream. This course 'called' to me. I excitedly sent in a letter of application together with my deposit and expected to hear from Jayem, the course presenter, the next day. This was not the case. I waited eagerly and impatiently, looking through my e-mails many times over the next few days. Then I sent an enquiry asking if I had been accepted, but still there was no reply. After the third note and noticing that the deposit had not been drawn from my account I figured that this was not to be. Jayem did say that only some were accepted.

While all this was going on, and it was all within the space of a few days, my entire being was telling me to go to Ayers Rock, except my mind was saying no. I had no real desire to go to Ayers Rock. I saw it as a red rock in the desert! When I had no reply from Jayem I gave in to the Rainbow Serpent energy.

The day I got back from Central Australia, I received an e-mail from the co-ordinator of the events at the ashram in Bali, confirming my arrival at the ashram.

I was exhausted. Did I mention that I do not like camping? I like a warm bed and I like lights. So sleeping on a camp bed, in a slippery sleeping bag, trying to wind up those camp torches to get a glimmer of light, to find the torch that I'd left somewhere on the bedside table to go to the toilet which was across the park was . . . . mmmmh challenging. The first night was spent tossing and turning in the dark, dropping my elusive travel pillow many times until it was lost all together somewhere beneath my U shaped bed. I could hear the snoring of the girl in the next tent. She had fallen asleep within a few minutes. Then I could hear the howling of the dingoes and there was a huge spider lurking in the corner of the tent. My mind complained childishly throughout the night even though I was trying hard to say mantras to stop my silliness. So much for being pious and pure! Then I heard a clear question, "What do you want?"

"I want a proper bed and room," I cried.

To return to the course I wanted to do in Bali, I wrote back to tell Sandy, the events manager, that since I had not heard from them I had gone on another trip and had only just got back that morning. I had left my son, who was in Year 12 for a week already and I was not ready to go anywhere again, just yet. He had gotten up late a couple of mornings while I was away and missed a few morning sessions at school. I was not happy about this but I usually wake him up every morning and I felt responsible for his missing school.

Sandy then forwarded all the e-mails that both she and Jayem had sent to me, none of which I had received. The dates on them were proof that she did in fact send them. I can only conclude that a Higher Wisdom had stopped them from reaching me until I had made the trip to Ayers Rock. I wrote back to her and said that I needed to pray and would let her know what my answer would be in the next few days. The course was to start in about two weeks.

That night my mother had a dream. In the dream she saw a snake fighting an elephant. Then another elephant comes to help the first elephant and the snake seems to have to fight both. When she repeated the dream to me, she saw the two elephants as Lord Ganesha warding off the evil snake. But as I continued to think about the dream it felt like the snake was my budding spirituality and the two elephants were the many obstacles I was confronted with.

I needed to buy a new car because the old one was written off by my insurance company because of hail damage. This was quite unexpected and the money the insurance was paying was certainly not enough for a good reliable car for me. The sudden trip to Uluru had taken up quite a bit of my savings and the course in Bali was not cheap. I also did not want to leave my sons again. So between family responsibilities, concerns about finance and my need to follow my inner guidance, many elephants were indeed rearing their heads.

I received a strong inner message to pray. So I did. Soon after the answer came from my son who encouraged me to go to Bali, saying, "You listened when you went to Ayers Rock and you know what happened, so you must listen again."

Then my mother said that she would see to the boys and that I should go. Knowing that she would be a presence in the house while I was gone and my boys would have their meals cooked eased a lot of my concerns. Of-course I knew that my boys at 17 and 22 were hardly children any more and a house without Mum was hardly a time of great distress for them! No housecleaning for two weeks, yippee!!!

The Palpable Forgiveness course delivered by Jayem was another step in the unfolding of the mystery. We had twelve in the group. I felt a deep energetic connection with some members of the group, three ladies in particular. As I got to know them over the course of the two weeks I learned that one of them, the 70year old Australian woman, had many experiences with Sai Baba and had been to the ashram as well. She had experienced visions of Baba in her living room when her daughter was ill. Her story seemed to be parallel to mine. She and I had very similar life experiences. Talking to her helped me identify flaws in my thinking and see more clearly how messages from childhood and religious teachings have been the source of so much pain and suffering. Misguided religious teachings, once it has found a holding within you, is very difficult to untangle. Hers was Catholicism, mine was Hinduism.

I do not say that religion is wrong because I believe that the essence of all religions teach love and oneness with God. The teachings however, have often been misinterpreted and have dire consequences on mass consciousness.

Another group member was a woman from England. When she went through a healing process I felt the pain as clearly as if it were mine. I recall sobbing helplessly in deep sorrow across the room from her. At one stage in her healing she let out a guttural scream and it felt like it was ripped out from the very depths of my being. Later she told me that she was my mother in another life time. She is able to see past lives. The healing we were doing with Jayem seemed to have gone beyond this life.

Jayem, a mystic and a God realised-soul, is a skilled and compassionate facilitator who has a great passion for what he teaches and his wisdom is profound. In 1987, Jeshua appeared to Jayem and over the years Jayem has been an extraordinarily clear and humble channel of Jeshua's teachings. Jeshua shared that everything necessary for fully awakening in Christ Mind had been offered to anyone willing to live what He offered in the *Way of Mastery Course*. Jayem follows no schedule but just his heart and intuition while he teaches. He is able to tune into the group and seemed to bring up topics for discussion each day on things we were thinking or talking about privately. There were days when he started the class at 9am and then went on for seven hours with no breaks. I was riveted and absorbed every word he had to share. At times I could feel such strong energy in the room that it felt like there were many divine beings there with us. From this course I took away two things that have helped me immensely. They were: 'to make my home in the breathing' and 'to let each gathering to gathering be a new mystery.'

As Jayem says, "The art of palpable forgiveness is to discover what it is like to live fully in the present." If one trusts that our lives are divinely guided then each situation and each person is there for a particular reason. We need to treasure each moment and then let it go without attachment.

Jayem also has a delightful way of helping us see just how preciously divine our sexuality is. So many of us have grown up with fears and negative messages around our sexuality that feelings of guilt and shame linger on well after we have done many years of healing.

Sexuality is a sacred ritual union through the celebration of difference. An expansive movement of the life-force, it is the dance that balances, restores, renews, and reproduces. Sexuality is a profound rhythm pulsing through all biological life. Yet, we live in a culture where this element of our lives is either repressed or exploited.

In Hindu mythology sexuality is everywhere. Shiva is often worshipped and represented by his phallus, the Shiva lingam, a symbol which appears abundantly throughout India. Krishna was known for his frequent amorous adventures, and erotic images are carved everywhere in India. Sai Baba materialized Shiva lingams repeatedly for His devotees and Shiva and Shakthi are eternally making love. Among the Gods, sexuality is sacred. Why not then for mortals?

I recall floating in the pool at the ashram, clad in a beautiful Balinese sarong, thinking about Jayem's words that we are sexual divine beings. I was deep in thought contemplating myself as a sexual, sensual, divine being when I looked up and there in the sky, above my head, was a beautiful circular rainbow. It felt like a super-large halo around my head. It was so beautiful and so powerful. At that moment Jayem dived into the pool bringing me out of my reverie and I wanted to shout out to him that there was a circular rainbow above and God seems to be agreeing with me that I am indeed a sexual, sensual divine being and he was right. But we were observing silence for Shabbat so I remained silent. I shared my experience with him the following morning. A few weeks later, I read that when a circular rainbow appears it is indeed God's blessing and Him giving His approval of what is occurring at that moment.

The course ended powerfully with Jayem talking about the beatitudes and Jeshua's teachings. This course was like a vitamin tonic for my soul.

The following day I was to fly back to Melbourne. However, something felt incomplete and I was not sure what it was. I had loved every minute of the course. I had said goodbye to the amazing people I had connected with. I had bought books, DVDs and CDs to continue my learning. So what was it?

Later that morning I was having breakfast in the communal dining area, when my attention was drawn to a book by Richard Grant lying on the counter top. I flicked through it idly as I chewed on my mangosteens and papaya. I read without giving it much thought when suddenly I became aware that Grant was talking about the profound transformation he had after he met Sai Baba in India!

Sai Baba appeared once again like another bead on a mangalsutra. A Mangalsutra or Thali is a sacred thread of love and goodwill worn by women during a Hindu marriage ceremony. It represents a happy life, peaceful life, long life and a Divine life. The husband ties three knots on the string to show his promise to his bride; to help her, to guide her, to protect her.

Grant relates an interesting story of two brothers. One is in a mental institution and the other is a Guru who many worship as God.

The first brother says to the second, "How is it that when I say I'm God they put me in a mental hospital and when you say you're God, people love and worship you and you have thousands of followers?"

The second brother replies, "The difference is that when I say I am God I know that they are Gods too."

Respect all religions equally.
Sai Baba

Love and Silence

ONE DAY A WELL-MEANING friend decided to give me marriage advice. She related a story of how she and her husband had a very difficult start to their marriage and told me about the advice given to her. She was to ignore him totally and to answer him in monosyllables. She tried this and it worked so she continued doing this for the rest of her marriage.

That night I had a series of dreams again. In one of the dreams I am with a young boy in an outdoor theatre. There are several movies playing at the same time. We could choose to watch the ones we want. Then I notice that the boy I am with is being attacked by a monster in one of the movies. I tell the person to remember it is not real—just in your mind, like the Jumaji movie, and then it will go away.

The following morning I was very distressed with these dreams and with the friend's advice. How was what she advised not controlling behaviour? How can this be love? Can relationships like this truly be loving and open? It is manipulative and controlling and so hurtful. How could this be a teaching for me? Yet I felt it was.

The silence in my marriage had brought me so much of pain. I couldn't, for even a moment, think about ignoring someone. I pleaded with Baba in tears and deep anguish that I did not know how to do this. It felt like closing my heart off. What was I doing that was so wrong?

I got through my morning routine of preparing breakfast, school lunches and driving Desh to school in a haze. When I got back home I was so weary. Again a bout of sobbing overwhelmed me. Eventually I gave in to drowsiness and fell asleep and had another series of dreams.

When I got up the song, *Don't worry be Happy Now,* was playing on the radio. Just after I got back from India I had a dream of Baba in my heart and he tells me, 'Don't Worry Be Happy.' I knew this was a sign that Baba was aware that I was having a difficult morning.

The rest of the day was spent shopping, cleaning, cooking and paying bills and school fees. As I was driving home, I inserted a new *Way of Mastery* tape into my CD player and on it Jeshua talks about a big movie screen. Exactly the dream I had that morning. Once again I had evidence that my dreams were in fact messages and teachings from the divine.

When I got home it dawned on me that while I had been praying to Baba, Our Father, to help me be patient and to have faith and devotion, it really was Baba who was being patient with me. He was constantly giving me proof and evidence so that my faith and devotion would not waver and would grow stronger each day.

Many lessons were being retaught to me—this time in different ways. Just as a patient teacher tries to find new ways to make her students understand. It felt like Baba was reteaching me because I just was not getting it. So many lessons seemed to have gone completely over my head. So much I misunderstood and still misunderstand. There are so many paradoxes in spiritual lessons.

As I watched the Fifa Cup that night I prayed to Baba to not give up on me because most of the time I felt as if I was dancing with the stars. One step forward and 3 steps back!

Before retiring for the night, I went to my laptop to check my e-mails. A friend from New Zealand, Preba, sent me a picture of Baba smiling happily with the saying "The Will of God will never take you where the Grace of God will not protect you. When the hand of the Lord is with you no dilemma is without divine solution."

I include the prayer here because it spoke directly to my heart.

Dear Baba

I want to thank You for what you have already done.

I am not going to wait until I see results or receive rewards.

I am not going to wait until I feel better or things look better.

I'm not going to wait until people say they are sorry or until they stop talking about me.

I am not going to wait until the pain in my body disappears.

I am not going to wait until my financial situation improves.

I am not going to wait until the children are asleep and the house is quiet.

I am not going to wait until I get promoted at work or until I get the job.

I am not going to wait until I understand every experience in my life that has caused me pain or grief.

I am not going to wait until the journey gets easier or the challenges are removed.

I am thanking you right now.

I am thanking you because I am alive. I am thanking you because I made it through the days of difficulties. I am thanking you because I have walked around the obstacles.

I am thanking you because I have the ability and the opportunity to do more and do better.

I'm thanking you because BABA, YOU haven't given up on me.

Once again I received immediate confirmation that Our Father had heard my prayer.

Later that night, I picked up a book that I had been guided to about a year ago, the one the Lakshmi pictures were in, called *The Perfect Relationship—The guru and the disciple* and I turned to a random page. It opened to a section called 'The Secret Ray of Love'. The following is the extract.

When two people are genuinely in love, they sit very still. Because their love is true, it is free of desire and beyond the senses. True lovers want nothing but to be close to each other, their highest joy is to sit in inner absorption. They do not want to ruin that joy by talking, for they know that if they move or speak, their priceless moments of closeness will slip through their fingers. True lovers sit together quietly. They do not even say 'I love you' because that is useless chatter. When there is genuine love, there is no idle talk. Talking begins only when love is lost; then one has to keep saying 'I love you,' merely to inspire trust. To say' I love you,.' is not love, but merely an imitation of love. True love has no language. Looking at someone and silently emitting a ray of love, that is sublime. This is true and should be understood. Love is a secret ray of the eyes.

For me once again this was a teaching that the silence is not wrong, it is the intention behind the silence. When one uses silence as withdrawal and a means to control the relationship then that is not love. It is the very opposite of love. For control is inability to trust, stemming from ones own fears. On the other hand for love to be both given and received, silence is required.

Throughout this day I felt the loving guidance of a Higher Wisdom that seemed to have been watching me all day so closely, like a loving Mother watching and assisting her child who is just learning to walk.

While struggling in the spiritual field you should accept God as your protector. To instil courage in the child, the mother persuades it to walk a few steps but will be careful not to let it fall. If the child totters and is about to lose its balance the mother hurries to catch it. God, too, has His eyes fixed on the soul. The ever-present faith and feeling of certainty will bring conviction and fill you with Divine Love.
Sai Baba

South Africa, My Motherland, and Ubuntu

As I watched the FIFA 2010 World Cup I underwent a deep healing, grieving and learning. My emotions ranged from feeling so proud of South Africa, my Mother land, and Her ability to host so magnificent an event, to feeling that I had abandoned her in my fear when I emigrated in 1999. Then I felt how much more than a game this event was. It truly was a uniting of nations, in joy, disappointment, grief and elation. South Africa is called the Rainbow Nation, and it is no co-incidence that this Rainbow Nation which is in the womb of the world, Africa, hosted this World Cup which is a game that unites nations of all colours and creeds.

The depth of the love I felt for South Africa, my birth country was equalled by the gratitude I felt for Australia, my surrogate Mother who welcomed me and my family with loving open arms. My tears which lasted for several days wavered between grief and gratitude.

The Divine reaches us through music and sound. When we listen to a song and we are stirred by the music and words this is a sign for us to pay close attention to the message. Shakira, the pop artist, sang a traditional African song *Waka Waka* as one of the theme songs during the World Cup. Some felt that it should have been an indigenous African singing the song, but since we are all so connected, her singing the song was perfect to bring the message of the beautiful words through.

> "... *When you fall*
> *Get up oh oh*
> *If you fall get up eh eh*
> *.... this time for Africa*
> *This time for Africa*
> *We are all Africa*"

While these words can be interpreted as a message to the individual players and teams, it is also a message for the South African nation by the South African nation and when we go higher than this, it is a spiritual message and a reminder for us all. So the individual is the whole and the whole is the individual. The time is now. It is time for us to get up after the fall and take a stand together as one nation, one world.

The barriers between religions, nations, colours, and creed are being demolished. The barriers that caused so much pain, confusion, prejudice, conflict and ignorance are crumbling. We, who have been motivated and paralysed by fear for centuries are now being taken on and choosing to take the inward journey required for healing, learning and transformation. For when we heal and transform ourselves, we heal and transform our Earth. Our imperative is to rescue ourselves, from ourselves, by ourselves.

Personally this song moved me deeply and profoundly on many levels. I was recovering from a broken marriage and the loss of that identity, I was still assimilating the move to a new country and redefining my identity in this new land, and I was beginning to realise, with all the miracles and co-incidences that I was experiencing, that there was something much more than my limited rational mind could explain.

Another song that had me crying for days was R Kelly's song *A Sign of a Victory.*

I can see the colours of the rainbow
I can feel the sun on my face
I can see the light at the end of the tunnel
And I can feel heaven in its place
That's a sign of a victory

Now I can see the distance of the journey
How you fought with all your might . . .

Kelly wrote this song for the FIFA world Cup. It is a song of hope, courage and love—a song for all humanity.

A traditional African philosophy, *Ubuntu* refers to the essence of being human. *Ubuntu* speaks particularly about the fact that you can't exist as a human being in isolation. It states that no man is an island and speaks about our interconnectedness. The word literally translates into, "I am because you are and you are because I am!" and "I am what I am because of who we all are."

Ubuntu is also about living as one family and belonging to God. Your neighbour's child is your own and his or her success is your success too. It defines a process for earning respect by first giving it, and to gain empowerment by empowering others. It encourages people to applaud rather than resent those who succeed. It disapproves of anti-social, disgraceful, inhumane and criminal behaviour, and encourages social justice for all.

The concept of *Ubuntu* traditionally runs counter to the creed of individualism of Western society. However, we are now realizing that we must apply a similar approach worldwide. For indeed it takes a village to raise a child, and it takes a shared global response to meet the shared global challenges we face. We are truly all in this together, and we will only succeed by building mutually beneficial partnerships amongst global communities. This is at the core of *Ubuntu* philosophy: where all sectors belong as partners, where we all participate as stakeholders, and where we all succeed together, not incrementally but exponentially.

If all humanity could take a little piece of *Ubuntu* to their corners of the world, where perhaps with a little caring, it will take root as naturally as it does here, in Africa, in the cradle of civilization, we will see a light at the end of the tunnel, the sun on our faces, the colours of the rainbow and heaven will be here on earth. That will indeed be a sign of a victory as Paul Kelly sings.

While I was being guided to write about this African philosophy, I dreamt that I was handing out a book on Nelson Mandela to my son to complete an assignment. I knew that this was a message for me to read the book I had on my shelf. That same day, my niece who usually has no interest in what her aunt is reading, called to say that I should read a biography on Mahatma Ghandhi. So I read books on both these great leaders. All this was going on during the month of June 2010.

Then in September 2010, three months later, a friend forwarded an e-mail about the South African Sai group's presentation to Sai Baba in Prashanti, India.

On September 28, 2010 a group of 2500 Sai devotees from South Africa visited the ashram and presented a programme to Sai Baba. The concept being portrayed that day was the spirit of Ubuntu in South Africa. Essaying the beautiful story of Unity in Diversity, the fifty minute presentation ran through the historical time of evolution of the nation beginning from immigration of the tribal's, the Europeans and the Indians to the dark days of apartheid which concluded in what the nation was in the present times. The beauty in this presentation was that it was never said that these foreigners depleted or destroyed Africa. Instead, they proclaimed, "They were troubled times but it was these times that enriched the culture of the nation!" The episode of Mahatma Gandhi involving himself in the struggle against apartheid was also presented.

My need to share what I was experiencing was still strong, so immediately this e-mail came through I showed many family members what I had written about four months prior and what the South African Sai group had prepared and presented in India to Sai Baba many hundreds of miles away from me.

All the while I was writing about our interconnectedness, I was actually experiencing it. Of course at that time I was unaware of it,

I was just following my inner guidance. This inner Guru was in fact showing me that our connectedness is not some abstract concept but the reality of who we are. When we listen to our inner wisdom we are indeed connected to something far larger than the limited view we have of ourselves. The trust we must learn and develop is not the trust of some outside force but the trust of our own inner self.

Treat as Sacred the land in which you were born. Have patriotism to your Nation—but do not criticise other nations or put others down. Not even in your thoughts or dreams should you think of bringing grief to your country.
Sai Baba

The Grace of God and synchronicity

I AM FINDING THE GRACE of God and miracles all around. The divine seems to be answering my every question, every thought. This is done through songs, books, thoughts that pop into my head, e-mails, something on television. It feels like the edges are being sharpened and God is also erasing the errors, the errors in my thinking. The thinking that leads to me interacting with the movie screens in my life and being devoured by the monsters. I am being reminded to remember that I am that one who sent me forth. There is no I. God pervades everything. There is only oneness and what I do and think affects not only me but the rest of humanity too.

I see clear evidence of this on my cats. I have three beautiful cats. Lucky a ten year old tortoiseshell is extremely fearful of all new things. She was pecked by a crow about 8years ago and is now terrified of the outdoors. Gremlin, a very intelligent girl, is free willed and head strong and will not have her freedom restricted. As her name suggests she has two distinct parts to her personality. Some days you just know that you should steer clear of her and other days she is a purring bundle of love and playfulness. I am sure she listens to and understands all our conversations. The third cat is one that is known by many names. She's adorable, cute and loves human company. When I go through a deep healing and overcome an obstacle and fear I immediately see a difference in the cats.

One day, I went through a deep healing where I had to sit with and then overcome what seemed to be never-ending layers of fear. Then when I reached a place of peace within I noticed Lucky standing at the front door wanting to go outside. I ignored her and continued watching television. She, however, had other ideas. She meowed loudly and refused to be ignored. Finally I opened the door and she bolted out and rolled around in the sunshine. What a wonderful sight to see. She had not gone out for 8 years. She suddenly realised what she had been missing all these years.

These three cats represent elements in us all. The parts of us that fear because of past experience and also a defence mechanism for our body survival, the other part is the intelligent, free-willed self that is aching to break through any barriers around it and the third is the part of us that just wants to be loved and held and enjoys being in relationship with others.

My lessons continue daily. A dream that confused me was when I saw the vision of the car that I was to buy. It was a green VW. A few days later, Richard, my ex-husband by now, called to tell me that he had seen a car in Sydney that he thought I would like. The price was right and it was in a very good condition. I asked him what car it was. He sent me a picture. It was the car I had seen in my dream a few nights before, a green VW Passat. I decided it was a sign to buy it. However, I had not foreseen the complications of inter-state car registrations. When I took the car for a road worthy test so that I could register it, I was told that the car had failed the test and would need costly repairs before the registration. My immediate reactions were fear, confusion and anger. What did those dreams mean? How could I have misunderstood them? Then the message that popped into my head was that 'mere book knowledge is not enough' I must live it too. So I knew that I must observe these events and do what was necessary but remain centred. I need to use my mind to be aware of them. Desert wisdom operates all the time; we just need to be aware of it. This is consciousness. Ask spirit, feel the emotion, use the intellect and then act.

That night, 2/7/2010, I awoke at 2am with the song *Fireflies* playing in my mind. I didn't know the words of this song for I had not really listened to it before but the tune was very clear in my mind. Since my sleep had been broken I picked up the book I was reading, *The Upanisads* and turned to the bookmarked page. About two paragraphs into the reading of the *Shevtashvatara Upanisad* which the author called 'faces of God' I came across the following;

> *In deep meditation aspirants may*
> *See forms like snow or smoke. They may feel*
> *A strong wind blowing or a wave of heat.*
> *They may see within them more and more light*
> *Fireflies, lightning, sun, moon. These are the signs*
> *That they are well on their way to Brahman.*
> *(Upanishads)*

Later that morning I listened to the song on You Tube, and was amazed yet again at God's mystery and God's love. The words were so beautiful and so profound. How things work I don't know, all I know is that they do and I was being shown and reminded of the faces of God in all things. Once again I was being shown to trust my dreams and inner voice.

When I was in Bali a few weeks earlier, I had been sitting with a group of ladies late one evening talking about God, our experiences and thoughts when beautiful fireflies lit up the night. I exclaimed, "Oh look at those beautiful glow-worms!" That's what I erroneously called them. One of the ladies corrected me and said that they were fireflies—not glow-worms. Where these then signs that we were on our way to Brahman?

One day, I came across something on the internet on serpent wisdom in ancient cultures and I felt that I had to read that book. After searching through a few book stores I was told that it was out of print and the most likely place to obtain the book would be from a second hand book store. Then I got a vision in my mind of the book store I should go to. I was certain that I would find the book there. However, I could not find the serpent book but I did find a book called *Sai Vision* by Rita Bruce. Rita Bruce is a Sai Baba devotee who lives in the United States. Suddenly I knew that I had been guided there to get that book instead. It had been especially blessed by Sai Baba. I bought the book and immediately started reading it. I could identify with so much of what she was saying. She had been having similar mystical experiences from the 1960's.

To make sure that I was left with no doubt that the guidance I was getting and following was very real, later that day I received a telephone call from an uncle who lives in Adelaide. My uncle, a kind-hearted being, is a devout Sai follower and our family was tenants in his property when I was young. He monopolises many conversations with stories from the Gita and anecdotes of Sai Baba. This would be acceptable except he stops in the middle and questions his listeners and then announces their stupidity and ignorance when they are found lacking. I have been found lacking on numerous occasions. His view on my separation was that it was my karma. Apparently I must have done something bad in my last life and therefore was suffering in this life. He and I had very different views on the concept of karma. While he saw karma as payback for past sins, I saw karma simply as life lessons. Anyway, he called to tell me about a book that he was reading and he thought that I should read it too.

"What's the name of the book?" I asked.

"*Sai Vision* by Rita Bruce," he replied. I marvel at the mystery that is Sai Baba and the Grace of God.

> ### *The body is the field of operation; the soul is the pilgrim and the mind is the watchman.*
> ### *Sai Baba*

The Desert Wisdom Principle

When I started writing *Desert Wisdom* I received inner guidance to re-read a book called *Love of Conscience*. It was only when I took it off the shelf that I realised that Rita Bruce had written this book as well. I had bought this book in 2008 in Prasanthi and had read it on the flight back to Melbourne. Bruce says; "The title Love of Conscience is appropriate because this knowledge will teach us that we must change our established and familiar habits by first consulting our conscience before we take action." God speaks to us through our conscience, it is our direct satellite link with the atma, our divine inner self. Sai Baba says, 'Conscience is God.'

The Desert Wisdom principle is: Ask Spirit, feel the emotion, use your intellect, then act.

I knew without a doubt that the divine teachings and wisdom that was imparted to her was now being taught to me and I am sure to many more who are listening. For me the guidance and teaching was occurring through the many books, dreams, songs and thoughts. Often when I am in conversation with people, a certain word or phrase would catch my attention and I know that I would need to contemplate on that further.

Our thoughts, words and actions must be in alignment to bring balance and harmony in our physical world. Our actions must be guided by our conscience.

As Sai Baba states, "Conscience is God and that God is you." God is Love and that is our form, our essence.

Conscience is a person's sense of right and wrong especially in relation to his own actions and motives. This brings us on to truth and the notion of truth. In today's society our focus is on outside justice. Judging who is right and wrong, providing evidence to back up our arguments and suing and demanding compensation as an act of forgiveness. This however, has only resulted in more wars, more conflicts and more feelings of antagonism.

Instead of focussing on outward conflicts we should turn inwards and become aware of our own internal struggles. Facing an ordeal or challenge brings out either strengths or weaknesses within us. When we are faced with conflict, qualities of courage or cowardice are shown but it is usually the courageous qualities that are admired and remembered, like in the cases of Nelson Mandela, Ghandi and Martin Luther King Jr. Conflict, at its heart, lays the question of what constitutes right and wrong. Life challenges and conflict are not an aberration of human kind but is driven by the need to survive and propagate. We often think of conflict as major trouble zones in our lives but in fact they are just moments of choice. It is a part of life and growth. Challenges and pivotal moments in our lives cause us to look deep within ourselves and question our own behaviours, motives, moral fibre and belief systems.

However, that which we call our conscience must be closely scrutinised for often it is our imbued belief system, fostered upon us by those who came before. And because this belief system has been imposed upon us from the outside it is moulded by the fears, praise, admonitions and promised rewards or threatened punishments to be administered.

Because millions of previous cultures, societies, religions, rulers, leaders, and teachers and parents have been attempting to pass most of their belief systems on to the next generation, we find ourselves sharing a world in which there is a wide range of conflicting opinions, and our ability to listen to our own inner voice, our conscience, is all too often diminished. So an appropriate question for us to ask often is; "Whose thoughts and beliefs are these? Do they hold true for me in this moment?"

When we use the Desert Wisdom principle; 'Ask Spirit, feel the emotion, use your intellect, and then act,' we train ourselves to act from our Higher Selves.

Asking spirit is consulting our Higher Wisdom, our conscience. We need to ask spirit, which is our own inner wisdom. Remember we are the atma, the divine. God lives as us, in us and through us.

Then feel the emotion. Emotions are normal human reactions, linked to our senses. Since our bodies, the most important divination tool we have, feel these emotions, we should not deny this part of us. So we need to embrace it and give it the attention it requires. Emotions are our smoke alarms. They alert, warn and inform us.

Next the intellect should be used to explore the thoughts and emotions. This can be done using self inquiry and processes like radical inquiry or journey work. In essence, we need to use a series of questions to help us investigate our thought patterns.

Lastly, allow your emotions and intellect to guide your actions.

Another way of understanding the Desert Wisdom principle is: Asking our Higher Wisdom (Atma), then carrying out our Dharma (duty) by using the human elements of emotions and the intellect.

Using the Desert Wisdom principle at pivotal points in our life helps us to make informed choices from a place of clarity. When we make decisions based on our own internal wisdom, we turn inwards and become more aware of our emotions and we are able to use deep thinking to guide our actions. We are then able to act from a place of peace rather than react from of place of fear, ignorance and unawareness.

When we follow the Desert Wisdom principle, we are in fact ensuring that the body, mind and soul are working together in harmony; a holy trinity. This creates balance between the spirit and matter. Since we are spiritual divine beings wearing this dress called our bodies in this physical world, this makes for a peaceful and harmonious existence.

Our responsibility now is to turn inwards, and fight the foe that lives within. Who or what is this foe? Our own distorted thinking based on past experiences and belief systems thrust upon us by parents, schools, society, media and religion. Does this mean judging and abusing ourselves? No, it does not. But the only person we can be truthful with and to is the self.

The Self is the spark of the Divine and this is God. God is Love. Fear is the opposite of love, so we need to continually reflect on our actions and thoughts and see where fear lurks. For when we identify the fear in us we see where we have been untruthful to ourselves and where we have betrayed ourselves and have settled for something that has brought pain and suffering into our lives. Often our rational mind will say that we had no choice. But when you examine this closely and look for the belief system that is operating within you, the realisation will dawn that this does not hold true for you at that moment. Fear results in resistance, constrictions and doubts about our self worth. Often those belief systems that are so deeply entrenched within us are rooted in the fertiliser of fear. When our actions are motivated by fear there is no joy, no love, no peace and no happiness.

Practising the Desert Wisdom principle helps us connect to our inner being, thereby restoring peace and harmony within the self. Since we are all interconnected this will impact on all. So our responsibility to self is our responsibility to all and our responsibility to all is our response to the self.

Follow the conscience. It is above the mind. It is permanent. It is the voice of God, the voice of unchanging truth inside. Conscience is the soul, the spark of the Divine.
Sai Baba

Laws of the Universe

REMEMBERING OUR DIVINE NATURE, eliminating belief systems that were founded for generations on fear and ignorance; often by well-meaning individuals; and bringing awareness to our thoughts, allow us to understand our true nature and the Laws of the Universe.

A few days after I returned from Prasanthi I was given free tickets to see Esther and Jerry Hicks, who I had not heard of at that point. They were presenting in Melbourne on the Law of Attraction. When Esther and Jerry Hicks asked Abraham, who they describe as an ineffable Non-Physical phenomenon, a group of extremely wise and unconditionally loving teachers, 'What is the Law of the Universe?' the first law they were given was the Law of Attraction.

I believe that this knowledge is being imparted to humanity in order for peace and harmony to be restored on earth. The call has gone out and many have responded and many more will still answer. We are being reminded of who we are. No one is special in the eyes of God. We are all exactly the same, for there is only ONE spirit that moves through absolutely everything and everyone.

In December 2008, a relative returned from Bali and told me about *The Way of Mastery Course*. We then formed a group, which met weekly, and listened to the CD's and discussed and shared our thoughts. My dreaming had escalated to such a degree that I seemed to be doing more dreaming than sleeping and the books continued to come to me. I hardly put one down before another came to me. I can tell you I was not doing this consciously. I was in the process of separating from my husband, ensuring my sons were not disturbed, trying hard not to be terrified of finances, working a full time job and learning to cut the destructive ties between my birth family and me. My mind felt like it had gone into a spin. My life as I knew it had fallen apart. I certainly didn't envision myself at the age of 45 alone and all my beliefs being challenged daily. My mother and sister felt like aliens to me. They had no idea how to love and support me. I felt deeply betrayed by them. My mother prayed for my husband and me to reconcile and pretended to friends and relatives that all was well. I found letters written to Sai Baba kept at our prayer altar, the lamp, wherein she asked Baba to re-unite us. Most of the time I felt as if I was in the middle of a cyclone, trying desperately to find the eye of the storm. Often I was caught in the whirlpool currents.

At first I had not understood the full significance of what was being presented to me. Everything seemed so varied and unrelated. It was only when I was guided to write this book in 2010 and tried to reflect on all the experiences that I had and continue to have that it slowly started to make sense to me.

Two huge questions emerged.

Who am I?

What do I want?

Realising our true self and understanding and defining our desires enable us to live a purposeful and meaningful life.

For me, who I was and all the roles I played seemed to have fallen like old tattered rags around me. But in the midst of it all I felt that I was being held tightly and lovingly. So when fears arose and there were many of those it felt that they were immediately taken away. Often I had moments of deep anguish and grief and the sobs would erupt from the depths of my being but even then it felt like someone would immediately comfort me and the despair would pass. Soon I discovered that my suffering was caused by my thoughts and my beliefs and my refusal to listen to my heart. I had acted out of fear for so long. And so the process of eliminating the fears began. Fear has many faces and has many names. Negative qualities such as anger, aggression, pride, envy, jealousy, worry, withdrawal, rejection are just some of them.

The only way I could begin to know who I truly was, was to peel away the layers of the ego.

How did I peel away the layers of fear? I prayed to Sai Baba. I told Him that He said, 'Why Fear when I am here?' So I asked, pleaded, demanded, begged that He remove them. Often the fears were there and I did not know what they were.

One day I was helping my son with an English essay and we were discussing George Orwell's 1984. As I was explaining Big Brother's power and control I was suddenly overcome with a debilitating fear. God was Big Brother. He controls everything. We were being watched all the time. It is only when Winston (the protagonist) gives up and surrenders when he is tortured by Big Brother that he finally begins to feel peace, but he is a shell of his former self. The will that made him human, is gone.

I stopped the discussion in mid-sentence and could hardly walk away from the lounge to my bedroom because of the dark cloud that descended on me. I tried suppressing this terror but it washed over me like a tidal wave. I couldn't breathe. I stumbled to my bedside drawer and groped clumsily for my asthma medication.

I was terrified of God!!!

I was too afraid to acknowledge that, especially since I had been praying to God for years. I sat in this fear; I really was quite helpless to do anything else. At other times when I feared I prayed to God. Gradually I got the message, "God is you. God is you. You are God." I could hear this voice very clearly within. Slowly my terror decreased and my heart beat slowed down. I had read and heard that statement many times before but it was just an intellectual statement. When I had this experience it felt that a hole was pierced into a thick steel barrier which I had been so unaware of. Slowly my trust and faith in God began to grow. I was beginning to move on from just mere recitation of prayer to something deeper.

My growing awareness of the many co-incidences and the messages and guidance was making me aware that there was something far greater than me. This Presence was guiding me and helping me and loving me. All I did was pray to be strong and courageous. The realisation that there is this Divine invisible force operating both within and outside of me became more and more evident. I could not explain anything, even though I tried. When I just accepted that it is, and stopped trying to prove the validity of my experiences to all who would listen, I felt safer and more peaceful. Actually it's pretty reassuring to know we have this powerful team of loving beings helping and guiding us at all times.

The second question, "What I want?' proved to be equally as challenging as the first one. This one brings up all those feelings of guilt, shame, unworthiness and the list goes on. Identifying our desire is often accompanied by guilt and shame because we have heard in so many religious texts that we must get rid of desire. The word desire itself has sexual connotations and suggestions of greed and lust. Until we are able to recognise these underlying emotions and identify the belief or thought patterns attached to them, this question remains one without an answer.

For the Law of Attraction to work we need to identify our desires and know what we want. Only when we know what we want can we form an intention. An intention is a positive impulse. However, wanting is an energetically negative request. So herein lies the paradox. We must know what we want but the wanting is negative! How does one resolve this dilemma? We need to go one step further.

Every individual possesses a unique self-essence, and this self-essence is the fuel used in the creation of abundance in the form of a gift. To recognise your self-essence you need to know who you are. When our intention is an expression of our unique self-expression we offer our gifts and this creates abundance. Inform intention through the transmission of self-essence and entirely reverse the energetic polarity of attraction from a negative want to a positive gift. Give without the expectation of return. A gift of beauty is rarely denied.

So while we do need to know what we want, it is what we want to give rather than what we want to get.

Our gifts are inside our souls. Every person has a gift. Find it and abundance of peace, joy and love will flow into your life. Desire and intention begins the process. Your special gift provides the fuel. The desire to create drives the human spirit.

When we create peace, joy and love in our lives and awaken to who we really are and move into a heightened state of consciousness, we the human race, become co-creators with our God.

A native Hopi prophecy says; "When the Earth is dying there shall arise a new tribe of all colours and all creeds. This tribe shall be called The Warriors of the Rainbow and it will put its faith in actions not words." We are these warriors. We have chosen to be on earth at this time. We must remember this. The call has been made and our souls have answered.

We need to develop the ability to experience the world as a vibrant, seamless manifestation of the Divine. How do we do this? One method to use would be from the teachings of Jeshua in 'The Way of Mastery' courses. As a young boy, Jeshua tells how He spent hours of each day meditating on both inanimate and animate objects and tried to find the source of it. It is unfathomable. The unfathomable source in all things is God, our Creator.

God has no religion. God has no language. God is pure light, pure love and vibration. But we as humans use language and religion to express and share the feeling and experience we have with God. That never quite captures the true essence. It is like trying to describe the taste of sugar to someone who has never tasted sugar.

When we are true to ourselves and to each other in our relationships we align to our desires. Since the root of these desires is the voice of the Divine, our listening to this voice connects us to our divine selves.

You do not even need to read the Gita if you are rightly resolved. You will hear the celestial song designed for you alone if only you will call upon the Lord in your own heart. He is there, installed as the driver of the chariot of your body, as Krishna was the driver of the chariot which took Arjuna into battle. Ask Him and He will answer. Have the form of the Lord before you when you sit in your quiet place for meditation and have His name (the name of any God you choose) upon your lips. The Godhead will hear and will respond.

Sai Baba

Greek Philosophers

WHEN I RETURNED TO school after three months of leave in 2010, I prayed for guidance as to what I needed to do to extend my Father's love. I shared that I spent some of my time in an ashram. My students had many questions. What is an ashram? How do you meditate? Why do you meditate? Which God do you pray to? Then I noticed that while I was teaching the same content, the discussion that arose from these classes were deeper.

One day I was discussing Gods and Goddesses in ancient Greece, as part of the study of the text, *King Oedipus* by Sophocles. Since I was no expert on this topic I needed to research Greek mythology and philosophers as preparation for class. I had also given the students some homework to get them thinking about the topic. My intention was that the students would get a brief background on Greek mythology and understand the role of the Gods and the hand of free will in the context of the text, which was written about 2500 years ago.

The next day we watched a video on Greek Gods and discussed a few of the ideas. The discussion was so animated and thought provoking and the students asked some really profound questions. One student said that it looks like the Gods do not want to be questioned. For if you do, it is seen as arrogance, however, how will we know if we do not ask the Gods? How can we really submit to the will of God and have free-will at the same time, for having free will is seen as arrogance and pride and not surrendering to the will of God. I was listening, directing and taking part in this discussion yet at the same time it felt like I was observing it. During the class discussion I noticed that the students seemed riveted by the topic. I would love to say that I had this effect on them during all my lessons but sadly this is not so. I had this feeling of being out of my body looking down at me teaching and the thought popped into my head that Sai Baba wants me to be doing this. I did not have answers to the students' questions for these were the very same questions that had been tossing around in my mind. How do I surrender to God yet question Him at the same time? How can I choose to act yet know that it is only the Father through me who does all?

That afternoon, I received an e-mail from a Sai Organisation. An Argentinean Sai devotee, who is an expert on Greek mythology, talks about his experiences with Sai Baba. I knew once again that this was no co-incidence. I was being taught while I was teaching!

Dr. C.G Boeree published an insightful paper on ancient Greek philosophers wherein he writes that Socrates, the well-known Greek philosopher states; "The unexamined life is not worth living." Philosophy, the love of wisdom, was for Socrates itself a sacred path, a holy quest—not a game to be taken lightly. He believed in the reincarnation of an eternal soul which contained all knowledge. We unfortunately lose touch with that knowledge at every birth, and so we need to be reminded of what we already know, rather than learning something new.

He suggests that what is to be considered a good act is not good because God says it is, but is good because it is useful to us in our efforts to be better and happier people. This means that ethics is no longer a matter of surveying the gods or scripture for what is good or bad, but rather thinking about life. He even placed individual conscience above the law, quite a dangerous position to take in ancient Greece!

Plato, Socrates prized student, divides reality into two: On the one hand we have ideas or ideal. This is ultimate reality, permanent and eternal-spiritual. On the other hand, there are phenomena, which is a manifestation of the ideal. Phenomena are appearances, things as they seem to us and are associated with matter, time, and space. Phenomena are illusions which decay and die. Ideals are unchanging, perfect. Phenomena are definitely inferior to ideals!

According to Plato, the phenomenal world strives to become ideal and perfect. Ideals are, in that sense, a motivating force. In fact, he identifies the ideal with God and perfect goodness. God creates the world out of raw material, matter, and shapes it according to his plan or blueprint.

Plato applies the same principle to human beings: There's the body which is material, mortal, moved and a victim of causation. Then there's the soul, which is ideal, immortal, and unmoved and enjoys free will.

The soul includes reason as well as self-awareness and moral sense. Plato says the soul will always choose to do good, if it recognizes what is good. This is a similar conception of good and bad as the Buddhists have: Rather than bad being sin, it is considered a matter of ignorance. So someone who does something bad requires education, not punishment.

The soul is drawn to the good, the ideal, and so is drawn to God. We gradually move closer and closer to God through reincarnation as well as in our individual lives. Our ethical goal in life is resemblance to God, to come closer to the pure world of ideas and ideal, to liberate ourselves from matter, time, and space and to become more real in this deeper sense. Our goal is, in other words, self-realization.

Plato's prized student was Aristotle who was as much a scientist as a philosopher. What Plato called idea or ideal, Aristotle called essence and its opposite he referred to as matter. Matter is without shape or form or purpose. It is just stuff, pure potential, no actuality. Essence is what provides the shape or form or purpose to matter. Essence is perfect and complete, but it has no substance, no solidity. Essence and matter need each other! Essence, according to Aristotle realizes matter.

He foreshadowed many of the concepts that would become popular two thousand years later. Libido, for example: "In all animals, it is the most natural function to beget another being similar to itself, in order that they attain as far as possible, the immortal and divine. This is the final cause of every creature's natural life."

About the struggle of the id and ego: "There are two powers in the soul which appear to be moving forces, desire and reason. According to Aristotle desire prompts actions; however in violation of reason, desire may be wrong."

And the pleasure principle and reality principle: "Although desires arise which are opposed to each other, as is the case when reason and appetite are opposed, it happens only in creatures endowed with a sense of time. For reason, on account of the future, bids us resist, while desire regards the present; the momentarily pleasant appears to it as the absolutely pleasant and the absolutely good, because it does not see the future."

And finally, self-actualization: Aristotle says that we begin as unformed matter in the womb, and through years of development and learning, we become mature adults, always reaching for perfection.

My plan to do a quick preparation for a short 45 minute introductory lesson to the text, *Oedipus*, was not to be. Many hours and weeks later I was still being shown the links between philosophy, psychology, science, mathematics and spirituality. Just as we are all interconnected so too are all subject areas. We cannot separate subjects; they all have the same purpose; understanding ourselves as humans and understanding the world we live in.

If we imagine ourselves as cells in a human body, each with its own nucleus and innate intelligence we can come to some understanding of ourselves as part of a whole. Each is a vital and necessary part of the organism. None is more important than the other. Each cell has its function to perform. It is when a cell or group of cells stop functioning properly that illness occurs. In the same way, when we as individuals and as societies, stop performing our duties according to our innate intelligence we contribute to discord and disharmony in the world.

At a conference held in New Orleans some years ago, physicists were challenged to explain why there were no pioneers to the order of

Einstein, Bohr and Heisenberg any more. One young physicist pointed out that the comparison was a bit unfair. Those bold visionaries had been exploring the world outside, while his generation was faced with the infinitely harder task of querying; Who is the investigator? How is the mind our instrument of knowing, supposed to turn around and know itself?

In India it seems that this point had been reached and crossed very early. Fundamental questions about reality are found even as early as the Rig Veda. In the Upanishads this questioning is systematic and a relentless pursuit of truth, and it embraced the realisation that to know truth we have to come to grips with the medium of knowing and the identity of the knower. This realisation turns objective science into mystical awareness. While scientists and explorers made outward journeys and discoveries, we are being called to discover the science of being human by travelling inward.

In the Gita, Krishna talks to Arjuna about his duty to fight. He is a soldier but weakens when he realises that he would be killing his elders and relatives. Krishna talks about eliminating the evil-doers. Now it is our duty to be eliminating the evil doer, except that evil-doer is very much part of us. It is within us in the form of fears, vices and negative thoughts. In the Gita when the enemy was eliminated good reigned again. For us, when the fears, vices and negative thoughts are removed then love can shine unobstructed.

I think as souls we were determined to take part in the greatest shift of ages humankind has ever known. We have all chosen to be born at this time of great change to help bring in this restoration of love and peace and harmony.

We are spiritual warriors. Our mission is to restore and heal our minds. When we align and heal the body, mind and soul we then remember our God-Self and we experience the Divine both within and without.

In order for us to listen to music on a transistor radio we turn the dial to the right frequency. If the knob is not set correctly all we have is a cacophony of sound. Similarly when we become witnesses of our thoughts and actions we begin to fine tune our radios, our bodies and minds, and this allows us to connect to the right frequency, the voice of the divine, the innate intelligence that resides within us, our souls. For transformation to take place this is of paramount importance.

Science itself proves this theory in its double slit quantum physics experiment. When matter, in the form of electrons, was watched it changed its behaviour. Science and spirituality, like religion, are two paths explaining the same thing; the nature of man and his relationship with this world.

The body is mere rust and dust, the Atma is eternal.
Sai Baba

Realisation of Self

To know is the function of the mind
To act is the duty of the body
To remain the eternal witness
Is the function of the Atma
Mind, body and Atma
Together constitute humanness (Sai Baba)

THE ATMA, OUR DIVINE Self is our core. It vitalises our body to act and perceive, our mind to feel and the intellect to reflect and contemplate. The Self is the abode of everlasting peace and bliss. Yet we are so unaware of it. Both Baba and Jeshua and many other masters tell us repeatedly that we are that One. We are God, yet we find this so difficult to assimilate. This is similar to a young girl suffering with the eating disorder of anorexia. Since she has the belief and image in her mind that she is fat, no amount of persuasion can convince her otherwise. Only when she decides to change her thoughts and perceptions of herself, will she heal from this mental disorder. Similarly, we must use our minds to think, ponder and contemplate the truth about ourselves, our spirituality.

Another little anecdote that reinforces this point is that of the lady who lamented the loss of her precious necklace. She was in great distress and had looked in every nook and corner of her house. Finally, exhausted with her search she sat down in a corner and cried bitterly. Her husband finds her in this pathetic state. He enquires about the cause of her distress and she declared her terrible loss to him. Her husband was calm and composed. He looked at her rather confused and asked, 'What then is around your neck?" The lady glanced at it and felt abashed. She found that her necklace had never been lost. This, in short, is the plight of mankind.

Life's mission is to discover one's Self. We need to gain knowledge of the Self. We may take the guidance of saints and scriptures but we must put in our individual effort. This responsibility cannot be delegated for none other than you can redeem yourself. We are our saviour.

Humanity needs the knowledge of life to understand the fundamental principles of living, the spiritual laws that govern humans and their relationship with the world. Spiritual knowledge would remove the stress and the strain of life and would lead humanity to peace and bliss.

The world today is afflicted with binding principles and precepts. People are forced to abide by artificial rules of conduct. Religious dogmas and doctrines thrust upon the masses cannot bring about spiritual development. The way to go about it is to instil the knowledge of the inner self and this will eradicate sorrow and misery and ensure enduring peace and happiness.

An essential prerequisite for acquiring knowledge is awareness of one's ignorance. It is futile to try to instil knowledge into a person who firmly believes he knows it all. Therefore to acquire knowledge the shutters of learning must stay wide open.

Acquisition of knowledge is not mere cramming of information from external sources such as textbooks and teachers. We must educate our selves with the original truths in life. We need to study them, analyse them logically and then experiment and apply them in our lives. We can then accept those that prove true for us. The knowledge sinks in and becomes our own. Knowledge becomes ours when we contemplate upon it, assimilate it and absorb it.

The mission of every human being is to discover the human self. However, so often we remain sceptical and we question the authenticity of the supreme self. This questioning is not wrong. It is, in fact needed but we must do it with an open mind. We refuse to accept anything beyond the perceptible, terrestrial world because of our inadequacy for conceiving the Transcendental. When it was suggested that the earth was a sphere, the masses ridiculed this idea as preposterous, because it was obvious to the seeing—eye that the earth was flat! I think it is important for us all to keep our minds open to new knowledge.

The most rational, even scientists, would find it difficult to live in a world without assumptions and beliefs. We too must start the investigation of the self with an assumption or a hypothesis about the Self. That assumption is: 'I and my Father are One." Jeshua says this repeatedly in the *Way of Mastery* course and in all Sai Baba's discourses He emphasizes that we are not separate from Him. In fact Baba gave this mantra to His devotees to say daily to help us remember who we are.

SOHAM MANTRA

I am God! I am God! I am not different from God!
I am the eternal undifferentiated Absolute!
Grief and anxiety cannot affect me.
I am always content. Fear cannot enter me.
I am Satchidananda! I am pure Existence, Knowledge and Bliss.
I am Omnipotent! I am all-powerful; nothing is impossible for me!
I am Omniscient! I am all-knowing;
There is nothing which is not known to me.
I am Omnipresent! I am present everywhere. I pervade this universe!
I am Krishna! I am Christ! I am Buddha!
I am Sai! I am Sai! I am Sai!
I am God! I am God! I am God!

Self-Realisation is a paradigmatic shift. It is an adjustment of our perceptions, attitudes and beliefs. When we stop, reflect, ponder and contemplate upon the self and we use prayer to guide us along on this journey, we soon get into alignment with our true self and this leads us to our natural state of peace and joy.

Be your own guru; your own teacher, you have the lamp within you. Light it and march on without fear.
Sai Baba

The Vedanta

My teenage son and nephew argued endlessly with me for many years as to why I would say there is a God if there is no proof. According to them, "God was a propaganda machine used to control the masses," and "God is anything we don't have the answer for."

One day, August 2010, my nephew who by now had heard me talk about my many experiences and dreams and often raised his eyebrows at me asked, "Aunty Vasi, can you prove there is a God?"

"No," I answered, "I just know."

"That's not good enough," he replied.

He argued with me for three hours, very logically, that there is only this body. I realised, as I was talking to him, that my words were lifeless. Was I just a slave to the ghosts of old books? Had I lost my ability to reason and have an independent judgement? Was I just spewing stuff that I had heard all my life?

When I got home that evening, I found a book on my mother's bedside table called The *Vedanta Treatise*. Neither she nor I know how it came to be in my house. I picked up the book and felt strong energy running through my entire body and I knew even before opening it that this was going to be a very important lesson. I had no idea what the Vedanta was at this point. It was a teaching for me on the very questions that my nephew had interrogated me with.

I will try to provide an overview of some of its teachings as best as I can.

The Vedanta was originally a word used in Hindu philosophy as a synonym for that part of the Veda texts known also as the Upanishads. By the 8th century, the word also came to be used to describe a group of philosophical traditions concerned with self-realization by which one understands the ultimate nature of reality (Brahman).

The Vedanta presents the ancient philosophy that enunciates the eternal principles of life and living. Living is an art, a skill, a technique that needs to be learnt and practiced. The Vedanta helps you evolve to greater heights in your own spiritual path, it provides you with the knowledge and guidance to reach the ultimate in human perfection and the goal of self-realisation. It trains you to analyse, investigate and realise the quintessence of life. It reminds you not to submit yourself to blind faith, superstitious beliefs or mechanical rituals. Ultimately it leads you to spiritual Enlightenment.

Since the Vedanta is based on eternal principles, it is therefore a universal religion. It must be approached as you would mathematics and science, through logic and reason. The Vedanta equips you with the knowledge to make the right choice of action and it provides you with the techniques you can use in your home, business, in society, in fact everywhere. It gives you a practical way of life to satisfy your material and spiritual needs. You then can enjoy prosperity with peace of mind. The systematic knowledge gives you true insight, drawing you closer to your innermost core and reveals your real self; that part that is essentially divine, be you sinner or saint.

Those questions that my nephew had asked me, continuously for three hours, were being answered. I knew once again that those questions and the immediate finding of the book was yet another way that Baba was communicating with me. God uses any means to reach us. My distant learning course was continuing.

Before we get to know, understand and accept who God is, we must gain knowledge of the Self. We must inquire who we are, for we cannot understand the unknown God unless we start from a known. For true learning to take place we need to proceed from a known factor. At present, many of us do not understand ourselves. This ignorance manifests in three distinct phases: lack of information, lack of understanding and lack of experience.

In the first phase of ignorance we do not know the Self. We need to listen to spiritual masters or study the scriptures. This is known as shravana which means listening. Shravana helps you get over the first phase of ignorance.

The second phase is the reflection phase. The knowledge can only be understood deeply and absorbed through independent contemplation and reflection. This is Manana.

The third phase is fixating your thought upon the Self. The ultimate experience, realisation of the Self is gained through meditation, nididhyasana. From the balcony of the Self you watch the procession of perception, emotion and thought go by. You become the supreme Self, liberated from the persecutions of the body, mind and intellect.

To escape the persecution of the terrestrial world, you will have to learn and live the higher values of life. Living therefore is an art, a skill, a technique to be learnt and practiced. Unfortunately many of us live a good part of our lives without learning the technique of living. We often only turn to spiritual education when we have reached a crisis point in our lives.

For me, this crisis, the wake up call, was the disintegration of my marriage, my family, and my core values. Since I had placed so much value on family loyalty and love and defined myself by who I was within the family when this was threatened I was shaken to my very core.

The artificial veneer that I had presented to the world developed deep cracks and the ignorance that lurked beneath that, threatened to overwhelm me. The repetitive dreams of bathing and going to the toilet that I started having about the time I returned from Sai Baba's ashram in India now made sense. The faulty belief systems, the emotional pains and trauma, the negative thought patterns had to be revealed and released.

What I saw as the greatest pain and that which had left me bewildered and utterly confused, was in fact, my greatest gift. It was a wake up call to come home to who I really was.

Faith in yourself and faith in God are identical.
Sai Baba

Our thoughts

In August 2010, Richard who had been working in Sydney for six months as a computer programmer and had already started another relationship, returned home because his contract had come to an end and while he was looking for another job he was back home with the boys and me. I was thrown into complete turmoil once again.

I had started to gain a sense of peace and felt strong enough to know that I would be okay on my own. How could I insist that he go elsewhere when he had no income? Twenty-four year old habits and patterns are hard to break.

Our family had already moved from South Africa to New Zealand, then on to Australia. We had moved houses about five times while the boys were growing up. Soon after we immigrated to Australia we built our dream home. It was a huge beautiful home with lots of space and light and Richard had automated the entire house. However, travelling to my son's school took two hours each day. After three years of doing this, I was exhausted. The decision to sell our home and buy one closer to the school was mostly mine and I don't think Richard ever forgave me for this.

On the day we were leaving the house, we had cleared the house completely and then I did one final walk through with my sister. Richard and I were barely speaking. There on the kitchen counter was a picture of Sai Baba with the quote: 'Why fear when I am here?' Neither my sister nor I had any idea how it got there. We had cleaned the kitchen together and knew without a doubt that it was not there before. That was in 2006.

The new home was in a better zone, was closer to the city and served the needs of both the boys. The train station was close by, so D'Avery could get to his university easily and quickly and Deshlin could walk to school. It was easier for both boys to socialise with their friends. As an investment, it grew in value far beyond what we expected, but it was here that I experienced my darkest hours.

Now in 2010 we needed to make a decision about the home again. This time I was hesitant. I know that I can be very impulsive and I wanted to think this through. My head was telling me that I needed to separate from my ex-husband completely and the only way to do this would be to sell all our assets and pay off debts and mortgages. Certainly this was what a lawyer and all the women advice books were saying.

While I was fretting about this in school one day a student broke the silence in our classroom to ask, "Hey Miss, what would you do if you lost all your money?"

I looked up at her in surprise.

"Why do you ask?" I said, 'and what does that have to do with the *Romeo and Juliet* task you're on?"

"Oh. It just popped into my head," she replied. She went on to say that she would be terrified. Since that was exactly how I was feeling I knew that her question was no co-incidence.

The memories of childhood had obviously had a greater impact than I realised. Watching my mother work her long hours in clothing factories and my father ill at home, had left a deep imprint on me. While my mind reasoned that we never lacked food or clothes while we were young, I still had very deep fears within. I drove home praying on this and asked the angels to help me release these fears.

When I got home (31/8/2010) Richard informed me that we could lease the place and it would cover most of the mortgage! Not only would that release both of us from that debt but it would ensure that we still had something for the boys. These were the two things that I was worrying about. Why fear when Baba's here? Indeed.

Controlling and monitoring our thoughts is vital for our well-being and peace. Negative and self-defeating thoughts are like the entities in the film *Amytiville Horror*. When I was younger I had watched this horror movie and could not sleep for days. That film terrified me. A family moves into a new house and soon the dark evil spirits that were there start to cause havoc within the house and the family. The teenage son is possessed by a ghost and he eventually kills the family.

Our negative thoughts do exactly that to us, our relationships and the world. For world peace to occur we need to start with peace within the self and this starts with observing our thoughts and being willing to change.

Just as we spend a part of each day with personal care such as showering and dressing, vacuuming and sweeping and general tidy up of home and work areas, we need to monitor our thoughts continually. Thought is the substance of all things. It travels faster than the speed of light, Thoughts are instantaneous.

We are free at any moment to go silently within and observe and then change the thoughts we are thinking. If those thoughts are disturbing your emotions, then this is a sign that there is some vacuuming to be done.

For many of us, I know this to be true for me, it means resistances will surface. When this happens it is good, because it shows you exactly what needs to be changed. We need to become aware of it, and then have the courage to observe and change it. Use the Desert Wisdom principle or any method known to you. Ask spirit, feel the emotion, use the intellect, then act. Ask yourself as part of your inner housework; What needs to be changed? What is not working anymore?

Baba says, *"I have come to correct the 'buddhi', the intelligence by various means. I have to counsel, help, command, condemn, and stand by as a friend and well-wisher to all, so that they may give up evil propensities and recognising the straight path, tread it and reach the goal."*

As I contemplate the power of my thoughts, the meaning of the Lakshmi story, finally dawns on me. I received Lakshmi as a guidance almost twenty months ago and had been trying to make sense of that message ever since.

Lakshmi, the Goddess was first married to the demons. She is unhappy so leaves and goes to the God Indra. However, Indra is preoccupied with women and wine. Lakshmi waits for a while then leaves because she is ignored. She then enters an ocean of milk. She stays here for a while. When she emerges she meets Lord Vishnu and marries Him.

The peace-loving deity of the Hindu Trinity, Vishnu is the Preserver and Sustainer of life with his steadfast principles of order, righteousness and truth. When these values are under threat, Vishnu emerges out of his transcendence to restore peace and order on earth. Vishnu is often depicted as reclining on a Sheshanaga—the coiled, many-headed snake floating on cosmic waters that represents the peaceful Universe. This pose symbolizes the calm and patience in the face of fear and worries that the poisonous snake represents. The message here is that you should not let fear overpower you and disturb your peace.

The Lakshmi message for me was that I had to somehow save myself from those dark Amytiville thoughts and energies which were the demons. These thoughts had brought me great mental anguish. God Indra represented my attachment to worldly things and the eventual release of my expectations. The Goddess submerging into the ocean of milk is the cleansing that took place by eliminating harmful thoughts, beliefs and relationships. This cleansing occurs through knowledge, self reflection, contemplation and prayer. The marriage to Lord Vishnu is the realisation that, "I have Me and my thoughts."

As Sai Baba says repeatedly, "Don't look for me outside, I am You."

When I was young, my parents would take the three girls into the city to buy Christmas Lucky Dips. This was part of our childhood Christmas traditions. I absolutely loved these trips and the Lucky

Dips. Lucky Dips were special boxes with a variety of fun toys and lollies. We got ours from a furniture store called Models. The agonising wait in the long queues had me wriggling and groaning endlessly. Then we would reach the front of the queue and it was our turn to purchase our boxes. Oh, the fun and anticipation. I recall reaching in and pulling out a box of crayons. What joy! Then I would stick my hand in again and out came the fairy colouring—in book. Then the party whistle, the small rubber ball, the yo-yo, the ding-bat and the lollipop. Every toy was met with the same wonder, thrill and joy. Then the three girls would start comparing and this was when the trouble started.

Life and the mystery that unfolds along our journeys here on earth are those Lucky Dips. The toys are our experiences. How we choose to react to those toys depends on our thoughts. Experiences can bring us great joy or suffering. It depends on you and your perception of it.

The song *Cue sera sera—whatever will be will be*—sums up nicely how one should approach life. Most of our fears lie in our imagination of what the future might be. So our present peace of mind is destroyed while we worry about the future or when we start comparing ourselves with others. When we practise living fully in the present moment then we can have no regrets about the past and no worries about the future.

Our thoughts in the present moment create the future. Since your thoughts are creating the world you experience, it follows that you have the power to create your world any way you want. So, consider how you want your life to be. You could of course seek to make manifest the ego's worldly desires. However, this is not what Sai Baba recommends:

> *Man is wasting his life, night and day, for acquiring external things like houses, lands, vehicles, wealth, and other so called properties which in fact are not proper ties. Is it for the sake of these trifles that man is born? No, no, no. To realise God is his foremost task in life.*

> *Love is your nature. Nothing can exist in this world*
> *without love. You are the embodiment of love. Forgetting*
> *your reality, you are craving for mundane things. What*
> *you have to aspire for and what you have to experience*
> *and enjoy in this world is love and love alone. Other than*
> *love, nothing is permanent. (Sai Baba)*

Furthermore when Jayem channelled Jeshua, Jeshua had this to say to us:

> *Everyone has agreed to be here, and I come forth in*
> *this hour because I ask of you, I implore of you, drop the*
> *curtain of doubt.*
>
> *The love that it takes to remember love, to breathe*
> *love, to extend love, to offer forgiveness, the vigilance,*
> *the inner discipline if you will that this requires of you is*
> *far greater than it requires of us. We ask you then in this*
> *hour to come to see that you are the great masters. To each*
> *and every one of you, we have come to you precisely in the*
> *moment decreed by you before you took birth in this life,*
> *and not a moment before.*
>
> *You are the ones that experience a dimension in*
> *which you simply walk down the street, and you are*
> *bombarded by the frequencies of pain, frequencies of*
> *guilt, the vibrations of heaviness and doubt. Know you*
> *those feelings? You go to what you call the coffee-shop and*
> *you suddenly feel the heaviness in your auric field. You*
> *don't know where it came from. It's in the air. You are*
> *the ones who have chosen to incarnate in a physical form*
> *that shares the vibrational field of all of humanity. This*
> *means that where the body is that you once mistakenly*
> *called "me" or "I" is ceaselessly and constantly enmeshed*
> *if you will, engaged in the vibrational frequencies of all of*
> *humanity. Humanity lives in every cell of your body.*
>
> *Take a breath. For well did I notice the thought in a*
> *few of you, this sounds like a burden.*
>
> *It's not a burden; it is a blessing. Thank God humanity*
> *is in the nucleus of every cell of your body. Do you need to*
> *travel to the ends of the earth to help heal humanity? Well,*

your body may travel to the ends of the earth if the Father sends you. But the point we want you to understand, to take deeply into your being, to know profoundly; that every single moment you can breathe light into humanity, to every being, and every body, and every man, and every woman, and every child. They live in you.

How precious that is every moment, to be right where you are, to recognize that your body encompasses and carries the life of every being and every physical form, every body that has come to take on certain vibrational patterns, and there are certain beings that haven't got a clue how to breathe light into the nucleus of their cells. You can do it for them and rest assured when you simply remember the truth of who you are, and why you have come, and breathe that light and those frequencies, and you allow us, and you call to us to join with you in any given moment.

You don't have to go to a temple, you don't need to sit on a meditation cushion. You can go to your coffee shop for a whole new reason. Wherever you are, now is the time.

This is how we would ask that you do this. Any time you want, just pause and ask yourself, "As the arisen Christ, what Divine frequency would I love to transmit to humanity?" (Jeshua as channeled by Jayem)

Sai Baba has stated repeatedly that:

You are the God of this universe. You are creating the whole universe and drawing it in. You yourself are the Divine principle. You are endowed with immense power. The body itself is of limited power but your power is limitless, for you are the 'Infinite Imperishable'.

All that you see in the external world is present in you. The mountains, oceans, cities, villages, etc are present in your heart. All beings are you. You are the basis of everything. What you think is outside is only a reflection of your own inner being.

Vasantha Lakshmi Sai

One sees only a reflection of one's self in the outer world . . . Change your outlook and the world will appear differently. (Sai Baba)

The best way to love God is to love all and serve all. Your entire life will be sanctified thereby.
Sai Baba

Acquisition to Application

It FEELS LIKE I have now gone from the acquisition of knowledge stage of my learning to the applying stage.

As the days pass I notice that my thoughts and my feelings are not mine alone. I am experiencing what it is to be part of a mass consciousness.

The source of my guidance and messages seems to have changed from books and dreams to anecdotes and words in conversations.

A friend related an incident of something that happened to her at work. Her boss had asked her out to lunch. Since this was out of character and he was being secretive about the reason for the lunch she had no idea what it was about. So for two days her mind ran havoc. She imagined being fired, then she thought that he wanted to ask her about a fellow worker, a friend of hers, who was about to be made redundant. Finally she concluded that he might be interested in her romantically. She had very little sleep for two days. When the day of the lunch finally arrived it turned out that the boss had invited her to lunch to present her with a cheque of $500 as a service award. So instead of waiting with the eagerness of a child, her thoughts had caused her great suffering.

How well I knew this. How often had my thoughts had a life all of its own and caused me great pain and suffering. I was being reminded to practise this. I needed to practise being in the moment and to anticipate and receive each moment with the joy of a child.

There are wonders and miracles in each moment. I need to become aware of them.

Another anecdote that struck a cord within me was one where another friend asked his three brothers for financial help but only two of them were able to assist him. However, instead of accepting and being grateful for the help from the two he was very distressed that the third one had refused his call for assistance. He was offended and hurt and felt that this brother did not care. He then went further and told his oldest sibling that he had helped too much and that it was not necessary! This, of-course sparked another row. He had asked for help and was now putting conditions on who he received from and how much he received.

I sighed while listening to this because I knew that this is what I do and what so many of us do, in fact. We ask God for help and then feel that our prayers have not been answered or it has not been answered exactly as we wanted it. We miss the gifts by trying to control the outcomes.

A few days later I was having lunch in my staffroom and was looking idly through the window at the students. I noticed a dishevelled student-teacher walk by. For some reason I was propelled to get up and pop my head around the corner just to have a closer look at him. As he walked through the door, two year nine boys walked out. They were talking as many Australian boys do, with many profanities in their exchange. The student-teacher felt that they were swearing at him and confronted them very aggressively. I was so surprised by his reactions because I was right there as the observer and had witnessed the whole incident. He felt that they were being rude because he was Chinese. Even though the students' language was nothing to rave about, they really had no malicious intent however he was very sensitive. Suddenly I knew that this too was a lesson for me. He was acting out a part I had played many times before. Since I was so sensitive I took so many things personally, things that should really have just washed off my shoulders.

Dale, a kinesiologist once said to me, "Vasi you feel things 70% more than others. That's just the way you are energetically."

I asked him, "What should I do to make it better?'

He replied, "Nothing."

Learning to balance my energetic body, the chakras, and monitoring my thinking by using the Desert Wisdom principle has helped me not take things personally and has certainly contributed to a more peaceful and happier life.

Sometimes I feel that people cannot lie in my presence. It is the oddest observation that I am making. I am not doing anything consciously. The more I heal and listen honestly to my heart the greater the effect it has on others. They seem to reveal things or say things so they can hear themselves. Well, that's how it feels to me. These revelations seem to be just for them.

Nothing's really changed in my physical environment. I still teach at the same school, I still rush home to cook and clean and be a mother to my boys who seem to need me less and less in the ways of the past and I still have my 81 year old mother pray for the return of my ex-husband. I have learnt how to use B-Pay and the finances are not terrifying me anymore! Something has changed in my mind. I have become more aware of how I react and how I think. I seem to listen to myself talk. I sometimes have a need to withdraw and sit quietly in meditation and I sink deeper and deeper into this. I am still unable to meditate for long periods, so I allow my body to tell me what it needs and wants.

While the books I am being guided to are decreasing, the message I am receiving now is: 'Apply the knowledge.'

This week a student in one of my classes came to my notice. He had been absent from school for over two weeks and any attempt to contact home proved futile. Then I overheard another student say that he had seen the boy on a bus. I questioned him at the end of the lesson but he was tight-lipped. I informed him that neither he nor his friend was in trouble but that I was sincerely concerned about the absent boy. I was. The next day the boy turned up at school.

"Where were you?" I asked.

"No-where," he replied sullenly.

"Why were you away?"

"No reason."

"Were you at home?"

"Mostly."

"Did your mother know?"

"Yes."

After a series of questions and monosyllabic responses, he finally opened up and revealed that his mother was schizophrenic and she was refusing to take her medication. She was seeing spirits and was continually burning incense so that the evil spirits would leave. The boy's mother had gone off with the two younger children and he had no idea where they were. He was afraid for their safety. The student was confused and terrified and trying hard to be brave. He was twelve years old.

His father had died of a heroin overdose two years before and the student was the one who had discovered the body in the garage. It seemed like my simple inquiry into his absence had lifted the lid off a steaming pot. As I listened to him I thought, "Wow, this is more than I can handle. I need to get in the experts, the school counsellors, the psychologist, the nurse.'

I informed him that I too wave incense sticks around my sons occasionally and I saw his eyes widen in disbelief or was it hope? If his seemingly rational English teacher was doing the same thing as his mother, maybe all was not as bad as it looked and felt.

I prayed quietly throughout. I needed guidance. I did all the things that were expected of me professionally. Filled in the correct forms and informed the right people but somehow this all seemed so meaningless and ridiculous.

The question that kept coming up for me was; How are psychics and channels different to someone who sees spirits and is labelled a schizophrenic? Are doctors and psychiatrists labelling something they don't fully understand? Similar to when the witches were persecuted in the middle ages. Are we medicating people out of ignorance? How is what I am experiencing not seen as madness?

The answer that I received was, "Fear."

When we fear our abilities, this fear manifests as imbalances within our energy bodies and physical bodies. This imbalance shows up as chemical imbalances within the body. Then our behaviour can be harmful to both others and ourselves. Fear. This is what needs to be eliminated.

For me, it feels like fear has fallen away. I have all the same issues going on around me, except somehow in the middle of this, I have found peace. I do not have the sinking feeling in the pit of my tummy. The other day it came to me that I had a triple heart by-pass, of the psychic and energetic nature. My immediate family were my hardest lessons and the most important teachers. I am now able to walk away or stay. I am free to choose in each moment. I try not to do things because I have to. I do it because I choose to.

I have Me and my thoughts. Each moment I am aware of how I feel, react, think. I seem to be observing my thoughts, words and actions continuously. When I say things that are not in line with my thoughts, they are so discordant they feel like a physical jab into my chest.

I feel like Sai Baba, the God within, took control of my learning and led me to this place of quiet and peace. I step forward each day in strength, knowing I am loved and taken care of. Mostly I know that I am that one who loves and cares deeply.

I know that for now I choose to be a supportive mother to my son who has his final school exams in a few days. I also know that when he finishes his exam I will move into another home so that I can afford the house payments and this will help me be financially independent.

There are a few turning points in my life at the moment—the end of schooling for my youngest, my older son wanting to spread his wings by leaving home and me moving out of the family home, into a smaller one much farther away. I look around at all my possessions and think I don't need any of this any more. They don't fit, both literally and figuratively.

Yesterday, I was chatting to my boys and then found myself laughing hysterically at something that Deshlin had said. How wonderful it felt. I find myself smiling and laughing more. For a long time it seemed like I had forgotten how to laugh.

Deshlin was relating another Bunnings incident he had with his Dad. Richard insisted on taking Desh on all his trips to Bunnings, a hardware store, because he wanted him to learn how to be self-reliant. Desh's main aim in life was to escape these life lessons!

On this particular day, Richard was planning on adding some cupboards to the kitchen and he took Desh, who was 16 at the time, along with him to Bunnings. Desh reports having stood there for six hours measuring, writing notes and comparing products. Deshlin described his torture very comically and I'm sure as they hear about my many episodes with Ayah, my grandmother, his children will hear about his trips to Bunnings with his Dad.

D'Avery, the older brother, insists he had it worse and that Desh gets away with doing very little. Of course Desh insists otherwise. I listen to their good natured banter and think maybe my concern and worry that they would be traumatised by our divorce had been unfounded after all. They loved their Dad and laughed merrily at his idiosyncrasies.

Somebody once said that transformation happens in stages, because if it comes all at once the person will surely experience a heart failure. If somebody told me two years ago, "Guess what is going to happen to you?" I would surely have had that cardiac arrest!

The last few days I am being reminded to understand deeply the saying; 'I and My Father are One." A few months ago I read an interview between Sai Baba and a devotee. Baba touches His stomach and smiles at the devotee and says: "I'm pregnant. I'm birthing Prema Sai."

Somehow it feels like I had been experiencing that feeling of Oneness with no conscious awareness of what it was that I was experiencing when I had all those pregnancy symptoms in 2007 and 2008.

One night I had a dream where my husband was holding an eagle as a pet. The next morning as I rushed to work I was shocked to find an astounding amount of bird droppings on my windscreen! It seemed like the eagle that had been in the dream had actually been physically there.

Deshlin has started his Year 12 exam and I am trying to do what mothers do when their children are under stress—be supportive and helpful or rather we like to think we are. However, he's not eating the nutritious food I'm cooking, choosing rather to eat cheese burgers nor is he accepting the help I offer with English and Literature, the subjects I teach at school. So I have stepped back.

Being able to love my children yet detach from them is learning for me. But when I do this, it makes all our lives more peaceful. I am not imposing my expectations on them and they do not feel the pressure and burden of not living up to what a parent wants.

I have noticed that anger as an emotional response has decreased radically. The things that used to trigger me don't seem to have the same effect.

I reflect on anger and rage as an emotional response. While anger is a normal emotional response to loss, frustration or injustice—either to oneself or others, it is an emotion that needs to be controlled and managed. At its worst, it becomes an intense, disproportionate rage leading to violence and abuse.

It is natural to feel angry if our desires are frustrated, if we see others treated unjustly or if our trust is betrayed. The key to acting in a peaceful way lies in shaping our desires and handling our anger creatively. In some circumstances, for example, the expression of righteous anger can be entirely appropriate. Anger is a good servant, but not a good master.

We live in a consumerist culture and often are encouraged to believe that material things are what matter and what we should desire. We are told that we shall be happy if we have the latest clothes, cars and gadgets. Our economy is built on consumption. When wealth and possessions are made the measure of happiness and success, people who are already disadvantaged can easily feel further excluded. Even those, who are well-off can feel that they are deprived of what society says is their entitlement. Exclusion leads to frustration, frustration leads to anger, anger leads to rage, and rage often leads to violence.

We are also told that we should strive to be strong, individualistic and competitive. School is often about achieving, getting the highest scores and getting into the most prestigious institutions. Competition in itself is not a bad thing: it can bolster the common good when it is based on fair play, shared effort and a concern for those who are vulnerable. But competitiveness with no rules and a need to win at all costs, undermines the dignity of individuals and the bonds of our common humanity. An overly competitive culture based on selfish individualism is inevitably an angry culture, because for every winner there will be a loser whose desires and self-respect are frustrated.

Both anger and peace are ultimately matters of the human heart, played out where humans meet—the home. While the home is often the place we feel free to express anger, it is also the place of hidden heroism. People struggle bravely with their anger, forgive one another for their behaviour and make peace in difficult situations. We are less aware of the courage of those who control their feelings, soothe the angry and try to find a better way to resolve conflict. Patience and strength is apparent in family members who struggle with normal feelings of frustration and anger.

For me, those two words is my message now. I need to practise strength and patience. With strength and patience comes living in the moment and trusting a Higher Guidance.

Deshlin is still busy with exams, D'Avery is house hunting and I am trying to resolve my living situation and work has become rather busy with the marking of exams and report writing.

In the midst of this comes the annual celebrations of Diwali and I have become one of Skinner's rats. Diwali, a special Hindu festival fell on the 05/11/2010. It is called the Festival of Lights and signifies the triumph of light and goodness over darkness and evil.

I am so conditioned to the rituals involved in this celebration; the week-long preparation of sweetmeats, the spring-cleaning of the house, the buying of new clothes and all the other little things that go along with it that I have gone into auto-pilot mode.

My sons ask, "Why are you doing all this?"

"For you," I reply.

"We don't want it," they say. "We don't eat most of the stuff. Also the house looks clean as it is."

"That's because you both have blinkers on your eyes," I bite back, the image of them calmly stepping over damp towels on the bathroom floor flashing across my mind.

"Can we skip the temple this year?" they ask.

I glare at them.

Diwali arrives and as is the way in many Hindu households, the mother gets up early to wash and polish the brass prayer lamp, cook for the day and clean the already cleaned house thoroughly once again. Then she mixes three types of oils and rubs this onto the heads of family members; an anointment. You would think after all these years the boys would be used to it, but they complain loudly and are horrified at the thought of oil on their heads. Apparently oil and hair-gel don't mix! The three heads have now been reduced to two and I feel a moment of sadness. The mother then makes a number of sweetmeat trays to distribute to family, friends and neighbours. All are offered to God.

After lunch, we drove to a temple in Carrum Downs to pray. While at the temple I was drawn to a pamphlet on a notice board advertising a talk on the Vedanta. It was to be held in the Shirdi Baba ashram that was close to my home. I noted the details and decided that I would attend.

The day of the talk arrived and when I got to the Shirdi Baba temple in Camberwell, I observed that a special prayer was being held. I sat down to pray and then I felt the strong presence of Baba in the room. Tears rolled uncontrollably down my cheeks. I was experiencing what I had felt in Prasanthi two years earlier. I could feel His love and presence so deeply. Baba's divine energy ran through my body and throughout the room. The energy and feeling was so powerful, I was in awe. It felt like a warm blanket around me. Then the men, who were conducting the prayer ceremony, asked the few people present to stand in a line and wash the feet of Baba.

He knew how important family was to me and there I was trying to make sense of my life as it was then. I knew I was heading for something new but the old patterns and beliefs were entrenched very deeply in my mind. When I regained some of my composure and remembered why I had come to the ashram I asked an attendant if she knew where the Vedanta talk was being held. She did not know but went on to ask the manager of the temple. He said that no talks were being held at the temple.

As I left the ashram thinking to myself that I had gotten the date wrong, I saw a replica of the notice I had seen a week earlier. I was in the right place on the right date yet no-one knew anything about the Vedanta workshop. How deeply I knew that once again Sai Baba had guided me there and I was given padhanamaskar, an opportunity to wash, touch or pray at the feet of the Lord.

As I drove home Bruno Mars song *Just the way you are*, plucked the strings of my heart and once again tears flowed.

A few weeks later Deshlin finished his Year 12 exams and I knew that it was time for me to move. I had chosen to remain where I was so that Desh's schooling was not disrupted. The move turned out to be a mammoth task that took two months to complete.

Open houses, lease agreements, cleaning and clearing, dividing possessions between Richard and me and trying to help two sons start new phases in their lives, became the order of the day. I would start my day at 6am and fall exhausted into bed after midnight. I was still in school for some part of this so that meant reports and all the busyness that teacher's experience. The move was finally completed when the new tenants moved into our home. D'Avery and Richard decided on sharing a place and I moved away to Tecoma with Deshlin.

It was about 11pm on the 17th Jan 2011 when I drove towards our new home which is about an hour away from the city. Deshlin was in the car with his earphones on and suddenly the enormity of what had and was occurring overwhelmed me. My home and my family had disintegrated. One son had moved out, my husband was now an ex-husband and my youngest son had finished school. No-one needed me anymore. Something that I had valued for so long had suddenly been pulled out from right under me. Deep feelings of grief and sadness washed over me. I drove in silence. I was thankful for those earphones for once!

Soon I had to stop for fuel. When I had finished refuelling, I walked tiredly towards the cashier to pay. As I approached him another cashier waved frantically at me to come to him. Since I was the only one in the shop I found this a bit odd but I walked over to him because he was so cheerful and smiley. God knows I needed something to smile about at that moment. I was exhausted, dusty, badly in need of a shower and feeling rather sad. He was a young Indian boy. When I opened my purse he spotted a little pendant of Sai Baba that I carry around.

He asked, "Who's this?"

I replied, "Sai Baba."

Then he laughed merrily and said, "I know, I know."

My heart lurched. The words he used sounded just like Baba. My vision was blinded temporarily by the new flow of tears. I knew that Sai Baba was with me and letting me know of His presence once again. The attendant then told me that he goes to Baba's ashram once a year and he had just come back from the ashram. He also told me that he received Padhanamaskar. Had both of us received Padhanamaskar on the same day? Me in Melbourne and him in India? When I left the petrol station I suddenly felt lighter and I knew that I was being helped, guided and protected.

While change can be exciting and wonderful it is also terrifying and daunting. I seemed to alternate between the two. I prayed for guidance and strength and courage but sometimes I could not hear the guidance. My emotions were pots of rapidly boiling milk threatening to spill over. I knew that I was going through another layer of deep emotional healing. I could not suppress the emotions and so I let them pass and observed them like clouds on rainy days.

The new school year started a few days later and it was time to get to work again. My holidays had been anything but restful, but the timing was all so divinely co-ordinated. I would not have managed the move if I was at work. It felt like someone knew my schedule and arranged things accordingly. I had moved countries twice before but this move was so huge that I knew on a subtle level something very large had occurred.

Around me Australia was experiencing floods and cyclones. The devastation was huge but the human spirit triumphed. I wept as I saw and heard about the kindness of strangers. I knew at the depth of my being that despite all our silliness and pettiness, we humans are really quite a good bunch.

I continued my inner work. I asked for guidance and went about my day. D'Avery, my elder son, seemed to be enjoying his new found freedom. Deshlin started his IT course and I had to get use to a new way of life.

At school I continued to feel the shift with my students. In my Year 12 English classes we were exploring the concept of Who am I? With my junior students I was teaching The Habits of Mind. In my Year 10 English classes I taught the text *To Kill a Mockingbird*. Martin Luther King and his role were intensely discussed. My teachings in all my classes felt like they were for my learning. I asked for guidance, and received the answer, 'Just provide the context'. I felt like God had gotten into the cracks of the Australian education system.

At times I felt like I was in a science fiction movie. If I had a negative thought about a student, immediately the student would react angrily towards me. Often the outbursts were so irrational that it would surprise both the student and me. I learned to watch my thoughts carefully.

One day I was doing a global meditation to send healing to the waters in Japan. It was to be at 12noon. Since this was right in the middle of class-time, I planned on asking my students to join me in this but I got involved in the lesson and did not have the time to prepare the students. One young boy was being a little silly that day and he made some deliberate sexist remarks that had both me and the girls in the class reacting. However, exactly at 12 o'clock, I felt a sudden surge of energy run through me, reminding me to stop and pray. I did this without the students being aware of what I was doing. A few days later I was with this Year eight class again and was teaching them the skills of letter writing. Suddenly, the very student that distracted me days earlier asked me if the class could write love letters to Japan. So even though I had not spoken to them about sending love to Japan my intention to ask them must surely have been heard. The entire class then sat down to write love letters to Japan. They spoke to Japan as if she was a person and told her how sorry they were for all she was going through and sent her their love. I was so moved. I knew that God was guiding them as closely as He was guiding me. No words were necessary; just love and intention.

The months past and I grew stronger and less fearful. My mind was more peaceful and a wonderful sense of happiness seemed to run through me. All around the world extraordinary events were taking place. There were earthquakes in New Zealand, floods in Australia and tsunamis in Japan.

Man's life becomes meaningful if he conducts himself fully aware of the power of thought vibrations. The entire world is suffused with mental vibrations. In fact, the whole world is the manifestation of mental vibrations. Hence it is necessary to direct our thoughts on noble paths.
Sai Baba

Prayer for Our Mother

In April 2011, I received a strong and clear inner message to do an earth blessing at my new home. I invited a group of women friends and relatives and I was guided internally to set the date for Easter Sunday, 24 April 2011. Some thought it was a housewarming party, and asked what I needed for the new home, but I made it clear that this was not my intention. It was to be a prayer for Mother Earth.

One relative had a dream of my garden and she saw two snakes in it and another friend had a vision of what I would be wearing. Since I had bought the outfit the day before especially for the prayer, I knew that something much more than my mere eyes could see was taking place.

I asked the women to bring something along to the prayer; something to give back to the earth. They were told to listen to their inner voices. The ladies brought seeds, blessed water, crystals, plants, a Buddha statue, prayer scripts and one friend brought along some gold jewellery of a deceased friend of hers.

For the meditation before the prayer ritual, we drew and painted pictures of ourselves as merging with the earth. This quietened our minds and allowed us to think about our relationship with the earth. Some protested with the usual 'I can't draw,' but we persisted. 15 women aged between 16 to 82 years sat scattered around the house and garden merging with the earth.

Then we sat in a circle, women from different faiths and shared what we had brought. My mother, whose name Jagathamba means Mother Earth, said the opening prayer. Karee, a Jewish lawyer said the *Om Namah Shivaya* mantra. Tu-Chan, a Buddhist who says she does not pray but whose actions when she lovingly picked up a worm and moved it out of harms way spoke far louder than any words. Gwen, an atheist friend who has a deep and profound connection to nature and the earth, and who had spent much of her young life as the church organist, shared what she loved best, a plant. One day, a few years earlier, I observed her reading a Dr Seuss book and she cried deeply at man's callousness and thoughtlessness to Mother Earth. All the women present were strong, beautiful, powerful women and the ceremony was so filled with divine energy. I cried through most of it. I shared a picture of Sai Baba, the one the American cranio-sacral therapist in Bali had given to me and a Shamanic prayer. The main message that came through was the importance of the Self.

When the last guest left after 11pm that night, I sat exhausted but happy and fulfilled, to rest in front of the television. A news-banner flashed across the television screen.

Sai Baba had died.

This seemed too surreal to be true. It felt like it was the 1st of April and someone was playing an April fool's joke on me. For the next few days I fell into the deepest depression I had ever experienced. What does one do when God dies? The depth of my despair is indescribable. Trying to reassure myself that God is the formless and not the form, as we are the souls and not the body, was pointless. They were meaningless abstract concepts. The tears flowed continuously. It felt like the end of the world. I wasn't sure why my body was still operating.

I chose to get up, and consciously made a choice to do what I needed to do. I drove Deshlin to a friend's house, I visited my sick mother, I cooked for D'Avery and did some shopping on the way home. The next day, I went off to work and continued teaching. My students asked me if I was okay. I replied, 'Yes." I floated through the day. I had a number of e-mails and Facebook messages asking if I was alright. I ignored them. I had no words for anyone.

Then the words of a Westlife song penetrated my blurry haze. My gut wrenching sobs came from somewhere so deep within and I had no power to stop them. My head tried speaking to me to say, "Really Vasi, you haven't even met Sai Baba physically. Get a hold of yourself!" But my sorrow continued. Then slowly the tears subsided and the sadness changed to a quiet stillness and finally gratitude.

This song and its message helped me heal from that grief and deep sense of loss. I include now the words of the song that helped me through the death of My Beloved, Sai Baba.

I was loved by you. Westlife

For all I've been blessed with in this life
There was an emptiness in me
I was imprisoned by the power of gold
With one honest touch you set me free

Let the world stop turning
Let the sun stop burning
Let them tell me love's not worth going through
If it all falls apart
I will know deep in my heart
The only dream that mattered had come true
In this life, I was loved by you

For every mountain I have climbed
And ever raging river crossed
You were the treasure that I longed to find
Without your love I would be lost . . .

Thank you Baba, My Beloved.

Vasi

Afterword

As I reflect on this journey it feels like I was shown a whole new curriculum; a universal curriculum which when implemented and practised with steady discipline will remind humanity of the truth of their original glorious selves. We need to be philosophical explorers of ourselves. Philosophers are seekers of truth and the nature of man, explorers are adventurers. This is the journey inward we must take; a journey to explore the truth of who we are.

The buzz word in schools for many years now is secularism. In our attempts to be politically correct and not offend those of different faiths, all references to God are frowned upon. The word God has become taboo. This madness in our education system is reflected in families, societies and nations. While our schools are cautious about religious education, which is understandable when one takes into consideration the abuses of the past, the students themselves have a deep yearning to learn something more.

The way to eradicate sorrow and misery and ensure enduring peace and happiness is to instil knowledge of the inner self. For when we get to know ourselves, we get to know God.

Epilogue

Guidance to write and print this book

I awoke at about 4am on 20 July 2010 with a message that I need to publish this book, but since I had written only 50 pages and had no idea where to go from there I dismissed this idea. A few hours later the alarm turned on at 6.15am reminding me that it was a work day. I lay in bed with my eyes closed for another 15 minutes contemplating the cold and thinking about the day. Then I heard the radio announcer interviewing someone whose father was sending him daily text messages with advice. The first one he got was, 'Wake up', the next day it said, 'Write something', the following day it said, 'Get an agent' and then it said 'Get a job'. The radio announcers were of course joking about the entire thing and they then asked listeners to text in their advice to him. A few minutes later he was offered a job as an electrician.

This felt like a message to me. This was what my Father wanted me to do.

About an hour later, as I was driving to school I listened to the announcer interview a writer who had published her own book and just to ensure that I had heard this correctly, during the day a student of mine came up to me to tell me that he was publishing a book. He had submitted it to be a publisher in the city who had interviewed him and now he had a time-line to submit the final draft. He then said, "I can give you his number." So in one day I received four messages!

However, it was almost a whole year later that I actually did anything about the completion of the book. I was awoken once again in the early hours of the morning on the 17/05/11 with another clear message to publish the book and the words 'You can do it' ringing in my ears. I went to work and about an hour into the day Karee, a friend, sent me a text message asking if I would accompany her to a 'You can do it' Hay House conference. I decided to listen to spirit and I attended the two day workshop. While I was there Doreen Virtue cards were handed out and I received an 'author' card.

The writing and publishing of *Desert Wisdom* is my response to spirit.

Bibliography

Divine Teachings by the Master Teacher.

I am in deep gratitude to the authors of the following books. Sai Baba, My psychic teacher seemed to have had your books under His arm and handed them out to me as I walked, skipped, hopped, stalled, ran, stumbled and limped through this amazing journey of discovery. Thank you.

My body would vibrate when I was being lead to a book. If I ignored it, it would come to me in another way, almost immediately, either via a phone call from a friend, a gift or it would cross my path again in some other way. I grew from a scared, unsure student to a more confident one. I loved this communication. Distant learning had indeed taken on a whole new meaning!

The books:

A Course in Miracles—Foundation for Inner Peace
Wheels of Life by Anodea Judith
Shakti Realm of the Divine Mother by Vanamali
The Red Tent by Anita Diamant
Think Positive thoughts Every Day by Patricia Wayant
Sathya Sai Baba and the Universal Reality of Mankind by Mata Betty
The Feminine Mystique by Betty Friedan
Tantra—Path to Ecstasy by Feuerstien
The Eternities Vedanta Treatise by A. Parthasarathy
The Upanishads by Eknath Easwaran
The Gita—the Krishna Arjuna Dialogue
Kundalini by Gopi Krishna

The Woman's Book of Dreams by Connie Cockrel Kaplan
The Secret History of Lucifer by Lynn Picknett
Entering the Castle by Caroline Myss
The Christ Blueprint by Padma Prakasha
Power of Shakthi by Padma Prakasha
Nelson Mandela Biography
Ghandhi Biography
Self Matters by Dr Phil
Relationship Rescue by Dr. Phil
Opening to Channel by Sanaya Roman and Packer
The Reconnection by Dr. Eric Pearl
The Way of Mastery Course—Jayem
Sai Vision—Rita Bruce
Love of Conscience—Rita Bruce
Cutting the Ties—Phyllis Krystal
http://www.cosmicharmony.com/Av/SatyaS2/SatyaS2.htm (The Lord
Returns)
http://webspace.ship.edu/cgboer/athenians.html (Greek Philosophers)
Songs by Westlife, Bruno Mars, R Kelly.
http://www.youtube.com/watch?v=KVUhcU7ghkA (Sri Sathya Sai
Baba)